Good Housekeeping

SIMPLE
and
STUNNING CAKES

Good Housekeeping

SIMPLE
and
STUNNING CAKES

GREG AND MAX

EBURY PRESS
LONDON

This book is dedicated to our Mums, Betty and Meg, for all their love and support.

ACKNOWLEDGEMENTS

We would like to thank the following people for their help in producing this book:

Gillian Haslam for her diplomatic skills and her sense of humour.
Marie-Louise Avery for her beautiful photographs and her Swedish stories.
Sara Kidd for making us look good (please!).
Thanks to Jerry's Home Stores in the Fulham Road, London, and to Leigh at The Scullery, Muswell Hill Broadway, London, for the loan of their beautiful tableware.
Thanks to Patricia Stone for double-testing everything, and then doing it again in plantpots.

First published in 1996

1 2 3 4 5 6 7 8 9 10

First published in the United Kingdom in 1996 by Ebury Press
Random House, 20 Vauxhall Bridge Road, London SW1V 2SA

Random House Australia (Pty) Limited
20 Alfred Street, Milsons Point, Sydney, New South Wales 2061, Australia

Random House New Zealand Limited
187 Poland Street, Glenfield, Auckland 10, New Zealand

Random House South Africa (Pty) Limited
PO Box 337, Bergvlei, South Africa

Random House UK Limited Reg. No. 954009

A CIP catalogue record for this book is available from the British Library.

ISBN 0 09 181433 2

PROJECT EDITOR Gillian Haslam
DESIGNED BY Sara Kidd
PHOTOGRAPHY BY Marie-Louise Avery

Printed and bound in Singapore by Tien Wah Press

CONTENTS

INTRODUCTION

Eight years ago it would have been almost impossible to imagine writing an introduction to our fourth book, and on cakes and cake decorating of all subjects. We have absolutely no training or qualifications in baking or cake decorating, and to that extent are no different from most people who enjoy making celebration cakes, or just enjoy a lovely slice of cake with a cup of tea. We love food in general, and cakes in particular, and so qualify as being enthusiastic at the very least.

However, since entering the sugar-coated world of cake decorating, we have been commissioned to make cakes for the Queen Mother's 90th birthday, for the birthday of King Hussein of Jordan, for the London première of The Lion King, for the 30th anniversary of the Habitat shops, and for a whole list of television, theatre and film celebrities. We have even taken cake decorating into London's art galleries with two West End shows of our cakes that resulted in an appearance on television's Wogan. There have been newspaper articles and radio interviews around the world, leading to enquiries from Japan, New York and Hollywood.

All of this is not just a big excuse for blowing our own trumpet (although we are quite proud of our achievements) but, more importantly, a way of showing that with a bit of imagination you can go an awfully long way.

When we first started writing books on cake decorating, we did meet a certain amount of what one can only call polite resistance. We were definitely seen as upstarts who had no experience but were suddenly causing quite a stir, and getting a lot of television and radio interest. We particularly recall being literally edged into a corner by a publisher and almost required to explain exactly why it was that we were on television, and their authors weren't.

After a time things became clear. We were suggesting all kinds of ideas, techniques and subjects that were simply 'not done'. We had broken a set of rules that no one had told us about. Having no background in formal cake decorating, we were unaware of the right way of doing things. This turned out to be a very positive thing. Without having to follow any self-imposed restrictions, we went merrily on our way, picking and choosing from any source for inspiration. We obviously struck a chord, because here we are on book four.

It often used to surprise us that in most cake decorating books the cake was almost completely disregarded. There was usually a brief chapter on how to bake a rich fruit cake, and sometimes a madeira sponge. There then followed a quick run through how to apply marzipan and icing before launching into what was obviously the 'meat' of the book – the decorative techniques. In recent times, at least some books are now classified as being about 'sugar craft', which suggests from the outset that the main topic is the decorative use of sugar.

In this book we want to place the cake where it rightly belongs, right at the centre of things. We also want to look at ways of decorating cakes in a much simpler, but often no less impressive way, and using techniques that do not automatically rule out all but the most ardent pipers, frillers and modellers. In our experience, all too often the hours of painstaking work that go into creating tiny royal iced details on a wedding cake go unnoticed. We have done a bit of highly unscientific research by asking wedding guests to describe the cake the day after the reception. Most find it almost impossible to remember the obvious detail such as what colour was it, or did it have flowers. We soon came to the conclusion that if you wanted your cake to be noticed, you had to get people's attention.

Given that huge amounts of time and attention are often given over to the arranging of celebrations, and also that they can be very expensive, it seemed rather sad that one important element, the cake, was going unnoticed. Even worse was the fact that something that had usually cost a lot of money had little more than ritual significance. Coming at the end of a meal, the thin slices of all too often dark and uninteresting fruit cake were consigned to the bottom of a handbag or a suit pocket, to be retrieved and disposed of at a later date.

We want to change all that, and in this book we have collected some of our favourite cake recipes. We have also tried to show that it is possible to turn a simple but delicious cake into something quite beautiful. We hope that some recipes might also challenge the accepted standard as to what kinds of cake are used for particular occasions. For example, we have taken the pavlova, that delightfully soft and melting meringue topped in cream and fruit, and turned it into a wedding cake. Similarly we have rescued the Stollen from its Christmas menu and designed ways to feature this mouthwatering cake at any time of year. Panettones have been brought down from the ceilings of Italian delicatessen, and been built into four-tier wedding cakes. None of

these cakes would be ignored or left uneaten, and in almost every case would cost a fraction of a more traditional centrepiece.

We hope that you will enjoy the cakes in this book, and have fun decorating them. Don't be restricted by our ideas. Just because we have used one particular frosting with one particular recipe doesn't mean that you can't choose another topping completely. Hopefully the ideas in this book will stimulate you to go on and develop ideas of your own. After all cake decorating can change your life, and we should know!

The ideal cheesecake – firm without being stodgy. Bliss!

DESIGN IDEAS

Thinking up an original design is simply a matter of looking at things differently, combining things in ways that you might not have thought of before, and being creative. It might be that it is simply habit, or parental pressure, that causes most young couples to choose a fruit cake for their wedding. Or quite possibly it could be that they cannot see exactly how you can arrange carrot cake or cheesecake to look like a wedding cake should.

The first part of this problem, namely how to arrange a cake, is a 'technical' problem and easily answered. By cutting lengths of wooden or plastic dowel, or sometimes even plastic drinking straws, that are the same height as the cake and then pressing them into the cake, it is possible to pile one cake on top of another.

Below: 'Cigarette' shaped biscuits are haphazardly arranged in a line over a deliciously rich chocolate frosting.

Right: Iced in white fondant and wrapped in a pleated white ribbon, this cake is completed with the addition of two ragged edged tulips.

The following six cakes are identical except for the way they have been decorated.

Above: Topped with fruit slices of different sizes and colours, this cake is finished with a glaze drizzled over.

This arrangement is referred to as American style, with one tier straight on top of the other, with no pillars in between. All that is important in this arrangement is that the cake should have a degree of density. This would not work with pavlova, for example. The meringue would simply be unable to support the dowel rods and keep them vertical.

The other part of the problem,

Above: Three sunflowers cut to different lengths emerge from a white fondant-iced cake wrapped in yellow tissue paper.

namely how to make a carrot cake or a cheesecake 'look' like a wedding cake does require a willingness to play around with a few preconceptions. Wedding and celebration cakes do not have to be tiered with cake pillars, and do not

Top: A white fondant-iced cake is decorated with swirls of brightly coloured royal icing. The red rope provides additional texture.

Above: The simple arrangement of plump summer berries stands out against the loosely piped cream covering.

have to be covered in royal or fondant icing. We have included several delicious recipes for frostings and coatings that are easy to make and apply, complement the flavour and texture of the cake, whilst at the same time looking just as romantic and elegant, albeit in a different way.

The important thing to remember is to take nothing for granted. For example, cakes do not have to sit on cake boards. As you will see from the cakes that follow, they can be iced onto sheets of glass, wooden boards or trays. The base used to contain the cake becomes part of the decoration itself. In our Sunflower cake the vivid yellow of the flowers is made even more beautiful by being seen against a gorgeous blue plate. Similarly, the whole philosophy of the Shaker religious group that gave rise to the Shaker apple cake is one of wholesomeness and simplicity, and the use of a pale wooden chopping board is a way of continuing this theme whilst adding to the beauty of the shimmering frosting and the deep red gloss of the apples.

Colour is enormously important in all our lives, but all too often cake decorators seem to draw back from exploiting it to its fullest. We were quite taken aback some time ago to be told by a well known cake decorator that when

Create your own palette by mixing colours together.

he first attended college, all the class members were given a colour chart. This chart was arranged in the form of a circle cut into segments. Each segment was filled with a particular colour. If we understood him correctly, the rule was that if the colours bordered onto each other, it was appropriate to use these colours together. The further the colours were from each other, the less they should be seen together. Presumably, if the colours were diametrically opposite on the chart, they should never be used together. The whole idea that there is a guiding princi-

ple as to which colours go well together seems to us to be nonsense. Who can possibly determine what effect you might want to achieve, or which mood to create? And for that matter, who can lay down such hard and fast rules seeking to over-rule one's own personal taste or cultural background? Limiting choice in this way would seem to be a recipe for mediocrity.

In all cases in this book when we have used food colours, they have been the dense paste colours, rather than the watery colours that are more often suc-

cessful with royal icing. The paste colours are richer, and you will need less in order to reach the shade you want. More importantly, you are not likely to change the consistency of any icing or frosting by adding too much liquid. Be courageous in your choice of colours, and in the way you put colours together.

Flowers are a classic decorative theme in mainstream cake decorating, but as we will point out

Add colour and texture to your cake by the creative use of ribbons and fabrics.

elsewhere in this book, the tendency has been, and possibly still is, to use small flowers in a series of small and tight arrangements. The sculptural quality of larger flowers, and the dramatic quality of some of them, is under-used. We have deliberately chosen large blooms and strong colours in our choice of flowers without using either rare or terribly expensive ones. In fact we have deliberately made use of an inexpensive spring flower, the daffodil, to show how different ways of treating this glorious flower can enhance any cake for any occasion.

Continuing in our belief that nothing should be taken for granted, we have also tried to show how the choice of ribbons and fabrics can in some cases do away with the need for any further decoration. The ribbon insertion method used in Aunty Madge's Christmas cake is one way of taking a tried and tested technique, but enlarging it beyond all recognition, and making much more of the ribbon's beauty, rather than losing it completely, as so often happens. Fabrics such as brocades and sari material or sari edgings can replace ribbon, or even be used to decorate cake boards.

Make full use of the fantastic variety of flowers available as single blooms or more formal arrangements.

∗Chocolate∗

CHOCOLATE

The scientific name for the cocoa tree is Theobroma cacao. In Greek the word Theobroma means 'food of the gods' – a fitting name for this most exquisite of foods. Having long been known to the natives of Latin America and the Caribbean, `chocolatl' was not even mentioned in any written form until the middle of the sixteenth century, in a book entitled *History of the Conquest of New Spain*, relating the conquest of the Aztec empire.

Montezuma II thought chocolatl to be as great a luxury as gold, and would serve the drink in goblets of beaten gold. Female members of his court were refused permission to drink it, due to its strong aphrodisiac qualities.

With its introduction into Europe, chocolate soon became a very fashionable drink, particularly at the court of Louis XIV following his marriage in 1660 to Maria Theresa, the Infanta of Spain. It was also seen to have certain therapeutic qualities. Cardinal Richelieu

Above: Ratafia biscuits, cherries and nuts trapped in a silky smooth mixture of chocolate and coconut oil.

Right: The soft sheen of chocolate is offset beautifully by the use of a gold serving platter and a simple length of ivy.

would take it to lessen the vapours from his spleen. Whilst the drinking of chocolate has been going on for hundreds of years, the eating of bars of chocolate is of more recent origin. It was in 1875 that Daniel Peter and Henri Nestlé, both Swiss, began incorporating Nestle milk into the existing rather rough chocolate bars to produce a delicious breakthrough in confectionery, and one that has travelled the world along with the hundreds of recipes that must have emerged since then.

As a general rule of thumb, the more expensive the chocolate the better the quality. In our experience, this does not necessarily translate into the better the taste. Choose a chocolate that you like the taste of and follow just one or two guidelines when it comes to working with chocolate, and you will have enormous, and delicious, fun. It is worth remembering that when cooking with white chocolate, it does not set as hard as dark chocolate. When melting white chocolate, be careful not to overheat it as it easily develops lumps. In our instructions on page 32 for making chocolate ribbons out of white chocolate we suggest that you melt the chocolate in a bowl over a pan of barely simmering water taken off the heat. This is not necessary with dark chocolate.

Be careful when melting any chocolate not to let water or steam get into your mixture. This will cause it to `seize' or tighten into a lump. If this should happen the chocolate can be rescued by adding vegetable shortening, vegetable oil or clarified unsalted butter a teaspoon at a time, until the chocolate is smooth again. However, adding any one of these ingredients will affect the proportions of the recipe that you were creating.

The careful layering of two kinds of chocolate ganache produces a striking and delectable cake.

DELFA KAKE

Not surprisingly we have quite a few friends who are involved in the food 'business' in one way or another, and also quite a few like Jane who simply love food, and love talking about it. Jane is one of Greg's oldest school friends, and recently we were discussing some of our favourite cakes. Jane mentioned this recipe as one that had been passed on to her by Mrs Saunders, who had taught Greg and Jane and who had remained a friend after their school days. Mrs Saunders, or Kirsten as she is known, has a Norwegian background so this recipe may well be of Scandinavian origin. Interestingly, and as if to prove what a small world we live in, Marie-Louise, the photographer for this book, recognised the cake. She has a Swedish background so the Scandinavian link seems established.

We did play with the idea of adding to the recipe by including meringue or macaroon layers, but realised this would only take away from the simplicity of the recipe and add nothing to this wickedly rich and melting creation. If coconut oil is not available, use a block of creamed coconut, although the result will not be quite as delicious.

This cake is very rich so small slivers are quite appropriate. If you want to make the finished cake thicker, simply double the ingredients and use the same size tin. You just need to allow it longer to cool. Once you have made the liquid part of the recipe, you can put this in the fridge to thicken before adding the fruit and biscuits. If the mixture is thin, the biscuits float to the top whilst the fruit and nuts sink to the bottom.

225 ml (8 fl oz) coconut oil or 198 g (7 oz)
block creamed coconut
350 g (12 oz) dark chocolate
60 ml (4 tbsp) brandy
2 eggs (size 2)
15 ml (1 tbsp) caster sugar
50 g (2 oz) lightly toasted whole almonds
75 g (3 oz) halved glace cherries

PLEASE NOTE: the young, the elderly, pregnant women and those suffering from immune-deficiency diseases should not eat raw eggs.

1 Grease and line an 18 cm (7 in) round cake tin. A loose-bottomed or springform cake tin makes removing the cake without damaging the shiny surface much easier.

2 If the coconut oil is solid in the bottle, sit it in a bowl of warmed water until it melts. If using creamed coconut, melt it in a saucepan or in a microwave. Break the chocolate into pieces and put into a bowl along with the brandy. Set the bowl over a pan of gently simmering water and melt the chocolate and brandy together, mixing occasionally. Allow the mixture to cool slightly.

3 Whisk the eggs and sugar together until pale and frothy. Whisk the coconut into the chocolate mixture a little at a time until it is well incorporated. Whisk in the egg and sugar mixture, followed by the remaining ingredients. Turn the mixture into a cake tin and put into the fridge for approximately 2 hours or until firm.

4 When firm, remove the cake from the tin and take off the lining paper. Gold coloured plates or plates edged in gold complement the sheen of the dark chocolate, and a length of ivy wound around the cake completes the picture.

DEVIL'S FOOD CAKE

It doesn't take much imagination to see just how a cake like this might

have got its name. It really is wickedly good. As far as we are concerned,

the pursuit of the ultimate chocolate cake is an entirely understandable

pastime, where even the noble failures are worth indulging in. Whilst this

might not be the `ultimate' chocolate cake, it certainly is a good one. With

its rich, moist chocolate flavour interrupted only by the inclusion of a

melting layer of chocolate cream, it is easy to understand how friends and

clients have always come back for more.

If you want to make this cake even more special (if that is really

possible), why not try sprinkling the layers of the cake with Tia Maria or

Kahlua before adding the ganache. You don't need to buy a full

bottle – a couple of miniatures will do.

100 g (4 oz) cocoa powder
350 g (12 oz) soft brown sugar
3 eggs (size 1)
300 ml (10 fl oz) milk
100 g (4 oz) butter or margarine
225 g (8 oz) plain flour
15 ml (1 tbsp) baking powder

For the dark chocolate ganache
350 g (12 oz) plain chocolate
300 ml (10 fl oz) double cream
2.5 ml (½ tsp) vanilla essence

For the chocolate ribbons
350 g (12 oz) dark chocolate
75 ml (5 tbsp) light corn syrup or liquid glucose (see page 30)

If you wish to decorate the cake with alternate white and dark chocolate ribbons, use 175 g (6oz) of dark chocolate and the same quantity of white.

1 Grease and line two 23 cm (9 in) round cake tins. Pre-heat the oven 180°C (350°F) mark 4.

2 Mix the cocoa powder with half the sugar, 1 egg and half the milk in a pan. Stir the mixture over a gentle heat until it thickens slightly and just begins to bubble. Be sure to stir the mixture continuously. Set aside to cool.

3 Cream the butter or margarine with the remaining sugar until light and fluffy. Add the remaining eggs and beat vigorously. Sift the flour and baking powder together and then add to the egg mixture a little at a time, alternating with the milk until everything is well combined. Blend the two mixtures together and pour into the prepared tins.

4 Bake in the pre-heated oven for 45 minutes, or until firm to the touch. Let the cakes cool in their tins for 10 minutes before turning onto a wire rack to cool completely.

5 To make the dark chocolate ganache, break the chocolate into pieces and put into a bowl. Place the bowl in a warm oven or place over a bowl of simmering water until the chocolate has melted. Allow the chocolate to cool slightly.

6 Put the cream into a pan with the vanilla essence and bring to the boil. Remove from the heat and gradually beat in the melted chocolate. Leave until completely cold. It is often a good idea to put the chocolate mixture in the fridge for half an hour to ensure that it is completely chilled. Beat the mixture very thoroughly (a food mixer is a real help with this, although it is by no means impossible with a balloon whisk). Beating the mixture lightens it so it will become much paler and will increase in volume. Ganache hardens as it cools, so either spread between the two cakes or split the cakes in half and sandwich the four layers of cake together immediately.

7 The finished cake is wrapped in dark chocolate ribbons. To do this, it is important that the cake should be filled and reassembled neatly. It is often a good idea to keep a little ganache back so that if there are any gaps or uneven areas when the cake layers have been put back together, the ganache can be used to cover any irregularities. Let the filled cake sit in a cool place for an hour or so to firm up before going any further.

8 Chop or grate the chocolate and mix with the corn syrup or liquid glucose in a bowl. Set the bowl over a pan of lightly simmering water and stir occasionally until the chocolate has melted. Remove the bowl from over the pan and allow to cool slightly. As the mixture cools it will begin to harden from the outside so be sure to stir every now and again. When the mixture is cold, knead it until it is the consistency of plasticine. It should not stick to your hands, although it will be a little oily. The chocolate dough is ready to use immediately.

9 To make the ribbons fold a piece of non-stick cooking parchment 30 x 20 cm (12 x 8 in) in half down its length, to make a pocket 30 x 10 cm (12 x 4 in). Take a piece of the chocolate dough the size of a small egg and roll it between your hands to make a sausage shape.

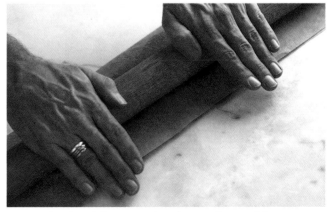

10 Put the dough between the sheets of non-stick parchment, and using a rolling pin, roll out the dough into a rough oblong. Peel back one side of the paper and, using a scalpel or kitchen knife, roughly trim the chocolate and cut it in half on the diagonal.

11 Take one of these pieces and, with the pointed end in the centre, drape the chocolate ribbon over the edge of the cake and down the side.

12 Take the second ribbon and slightly overlap the first. Once again, feed the ribbon over the top of the cake and down the sides. The chocolate will still be sufficiently pliable to shape against the sides of the cake. If it becomes too firm to bend, just gather it up and knead it again when it will become pliable. Continue in this way until you have wrapped the cake completely. Always trim any excess ribbons to the base of the board and use again. When cutting out your ribbons it is only important that the diagonal cut is completely straight as this is the one that will be seen. The trailing edge can be uneven as this is the one that will be covered up.

13 Make a rose and some leaves with any chocolate dough remaining. For instructions, see page 33. Given the richness and density of the colour of the finished cake, you might want to place it against another brighter colour to give some kind of relief.

CHOCOLATE LAYERED CAKE

There appears to be something in the very nature of chocolate that lends itself to excess. People who might otherwise never express any particular thoughts on sweets become quite discerning when it comes to their favourite chocolate. It is in truth so good, it's almost wicked. So perhaps it should come as no surprise to learn that in 1569 Pope Pius V gave serious thought as to whether the taking of chocolate ought to be banned during Lent, and that one Bishop of Chiapa attempted to excommunicate all those who might eat or drink chocolate during his services. Nowadays we can indulge ourselves without too much fear of castigation, and the following cake is dedicated to all lovers of chocolate.

But be warned – only small pieces are required.

A springform tin or even a loose-bottomed tin would be best for this, as it allows the cake to be removed the layers distorting in any way. When the cake cooks it will shrink slightly away from the sides of the tin. When you put the cake back in the tin, the slight gap created by this shrinkage may allow the ganache to obscure the cake layer underneath by squeezing between the cake and the sides of the tin. As so much of the beauty of this design rests on the crispness of the layers, it is a good idea to decide that this cake will have a definite front and back. Begin by pushing the first layer of cake against the side of the tin. After putting on the ganache, make sure that the second layer of cake is similarly pushed up against the same side of the tin, and so on. In this way at least one face of the cake is perfect.

225 g (8 oz) dark chocolate
100 g (4 oz) unsalted butter
30 ml (2 tbsp) caster sugar
4 eggs (size 2), separated
100 g (4 oz) plain flour
5 ml (1 tsp) baking powder

For the dark chocolate ganache
350 g (12 oz) plain chocolate
300 ml (10 fl oz) double cream
2.5 ml (½ tsp) vanilla essence

For the white chocolate ganache
350 g (12 oz) white chocolate
300 ml (10 fl oz) double cream

To decorate
cocoa powder

1 Grease and line a 23 cm (9 in) round cake tin. Pre-heat the oven to 180°C (350°F) mark 4.

2 To make the cake, break the chocolate into a bowl and melt over a pan of lightly simmering water. Stir until smooth and leave to cool.

3 Beat the butter with half the sugar until light and fluffy. Beat in the yolks one at a time. Stir in the melted, cooled chocolate. Sift the flour and baking powder together and fold into the mixture. Beat the egg whites until they stand in stiff peaks, then add the remaining sugar and beat until the egg whites are stiff and glossy. Fold the egg whites carefully but thoroughly into the cake mixture.

4 Pour the mixture into the prepared tin and bake for 40-45 minutes, or until a skewer inserted in the centre comes out clean. Allow the cake to cool for 10 minutes before removing from the tin and cooling on a wire rack. Once cool, slice the cake into three layers. Grease and line the cake tin again and put the top third of the cake back in the tin, cut-side down.

5 To make the dark chocolate ganache, break the chocolate into pieces and put into a bowl. Place the bowl in a warm oven or place over a bowl of simmering water until the chocolate has melted. Allow the chocolate to cool slightly.

6 Put the cream into a pan with the vanilla essence and bring to the boil. Remove from the heat and gradually beat in the melted chocolate. Leave until completely cold. It is often a good idea to put the chocolate mixture in the fridge for about half an hour to ensure that it is completely chilled. Beat the cooled mixture very thoroughly (a food mixer is a real help with this, although it is by no means impossible with a balloon whisk). Beating the mixture lightens it so it will become much paler and will increase in volume. Ganache hardens as it cools so use a spatula or knife to spread it over the cake layer in the tin immediately. Part of the beauty of this cake is the sharpness and contrast of the lines between the cake and the ganache, so be as neat as possible when spreading the ganache and aim for a completely flat surface, with no chocolate smudges on the lining paper.

7 Carefully put the second layer of cake back in the tin, pressing it gently but firmly on top of the dark chocolate ganache.

8 To make the white chocolate ganache, break the white chocolate into pieces and put into a bowl along with the cream. Set the bowl over a pan of lightly simmering water and stir occasionally until the chocolate and cream have melted together. Remove from the pan and allow to cool completely (placing it in the fridge for 30 minutes will help). Beat the chilled mixture thoroughly and use immediately. Spread the ganache over second layer of cake, once again being sure to be as neat as possible. Finally, place the last slice of cake on top of the white ganache, cut side down. The bottom of the original cake should now be uppermost in the tin. Press gently but firmly to ensure that all the layers are stuck fast. Leave the cake in the tin for about one hour to firm up.

9 Remove the lining paper and transfer the cake to a plate. Sift cocoa powder on to the surface of the cake.

10 If you wish, add a further layer of decoration by making a bunch of dark chocolate ganache grapes. Simply make up half a measure of the dark chocolate ganache. Put the mixture into the fridge to make sure that it is completely hard. On this occasion do not whisk it but take teaspoons of the mixture and roll it between your hands. To make this easier, coat your hands liberally with cocoa powder. Roll the ganache quickly and lightly into rounds and put in position on the cake. When you have built up the bunch of grapes, give them a dusting of cocoa powder if you wish. To finish the design add some ivy leaves, or vine leaves if available.

RICH CHOCOLATE CAKE WITH WHITE CHOCOLATE CRUST

This recipe first attracted our attention whilst on holiday. We saw it in a newspaper and wondered how it would turn out with so little flour in it. Two friends who tested the recipe for us said it was the closest they had ever come to chocolate ice cream in a cake. With its intense chocolate flavour and close velvety texture, it's easy to see why. This wonderful creation is then wrapped in chocolate ribbons and finished with chocolate roses. Don't be put off – it is much easier than it seems.

Corn syrup is available in food stores. It is sold in bottles and has the consistency of clear runny honey. If unavailable, use liquid glucose from the pharmacist. This is sold in tubs and is much stiffer than corn syrup. To make it easier to measure, let it stand in hot water until it becomes runnier. It might be helpful to bear a few things in mind when handling chocolate.

The chocolate dough will remain soft and pliable as long as you are working it with your hands. As soon as you stop, it will become more firm and will eventually harden completely. The chocolate dough will remain softer if left in the warmth created by a light bulb, for example under a lamp. If whilst working the chocolate your hands become sticky, wash them under the tap and then cool under cold water before drying. It is useful to have a damp cloth to hand to keep your hands cool and fresh. If the dough seems sticky, just leave it for a minute so it will be able to cool down slightly and will be easier to handle.

200 g (7 oz) dark chocolate
100 g (4 oz) butter
4 large eggs (size 1), separated
200 g (7 oz) caster sugar
45 ml (3 level tbsp) potato flour (available from health food shops; plain flour will do if you don't have potato flour)

For the chocolate ribbons and roses
350 g (12 oz) white chocolate
75 ml (5 tbsp) light corn syrup (if not available, use liquid glucose)
cocoa powder, for dusting
pink paste food colouring
pale green paste food colouring

1 Grease and line a 23 cm (9 in) round springform or loose-bottomed cake tin. With this cake it is a good idea to use non-stick cooking parchment, and then to brush the paper with melted butter and dust with flour. Pre-heat the oven to 140°C (275°F) mark 1.

2 Break the chocolate into pieces and put into a bowl with the butter. Set the bowl over a pan of lightly simmering water. Mix occasionally until the chocolate and butter have melted. Take the bowl from the pan and allow the mixture to cool.

3 Whisk the egg yolks with half the sugar until pale and creamy. Sift the flour into the egg mixture and whisk again. Add the chocolate mixture to the egg mixture and stir until combined.

4 Whisk the egg whites until stiff but not dry and add the remaining sugar. Whisk again until the whites are stiff and glossy. Mix a spoonful of the egg whites into the chocolate mixture to slacken it, and then fold the remaining egg whites carefully into the mixture. Pour the cake mixture into the tin and bake in the pre-heated oven for 45 minutes or until a skewer inserted into the centre comes out clean.

5 Cool the cake in the tin before removing. When the cake is completely cool, remove it from the tin and then carefully remove the paper from the sides. It might be best not to try to remove the base lining paper, but instead to lift the cake very carefully on to your favourite plate.

6 For the decoration, grate or chop the chocolate into small pieces and add the corn syrup or liquid glucose. Mix together to coat the chocolate. Bring a pan of water to simmering point and then remove from the heat. Place the bowl of chocolate over the water and stir occasionally until the chocolate mixture has melted. If you prefer, microwave on LOW for about 2½ minutes. The mixture might look curdled but don't worry – this is quite alright. Let the chocolate mixture rest without handling for several hours, or preferably overnight. It will probably seem hard and crumbly at first, but if you break pieces off and knead it firmly it will become smooth and pliable.

8 Dust the surface of the cake with sieved cocoa powder. Take 225 g (8 oz) of the chocolate and knead until pliable. This might be easier to do in small batches rather than in one large piece.

9 Take a piece of non-stick cooking parchment measuring 30 x 20 cm (12 x 8 in). Fold the paper in half to make a pocket measuring 30 x 10 cm (12 x 4 in). Break off 50 g (2 oz) of the chocolate dough and roll it into a sausage shape. Place it inside the parchment pocket and, using a rolling pin, roll the chocolate between the sheets of paper until it is about 20-25 cm (8-10 in) long, and about 7.5 cm (3 in) in height. Make the largest piece you can without damaging the chocolate.

10 Pull open the paper and cut a straight line along the bottom edge of the chocolate. With the chocolate still attached to the paper, lift the paper and position it against the side of the cake. Gently pull back the paper and leave the chocolate standing against the cake. Don't worry if the chocolate curls over or buckles as this adds to the character. Continue until you have used up the 225 g (8 oz) of white chocolate. You will probably find that you can wrap the cake more than once.

11 Take 75 g (3 oz) of the chocolate dough and colour pink using a small amount of pink paste food colouring. Do not use a watery colouring like cochineal as it will change the composition of the chocolate and make it useless.

12 Take a piece of the chocolate the size of a grape and roll it into an elongated pyramid, something like an upturned golf tee with the flattened end on your work surface.

13 Take some more of the chocolate dough and roll it out between 2 sheets of non-stick cooking parchment so that you can cut out a semi-circle about 5 cm (2 in) in length and 4 cm (1½ in) in height. Hold one end of the semi-circle against the base of the centre (the golf tee) and gently wind it around. Pinch the base of the petal to make the chocolate stick together. Bend the edges of this first petal back to resemble the centre of the rose. If you wish to enlarge the centre you can repeat this process.

14 The next layer of petals is composed of 3 semi-circles of approximately the same size. You will find that simply by handling the chocolate it will become warm and each piece will stick to the one underneath with gentle pressure. Fold back the edges of the petals of the middle section of the rose lightly. The final outer layer of petals is composed of 5 separate pieces, slightly larger than before. When the petal is fixed in position, bend back the edges and pinch to a point in the centre and at each end of the petal. Let the rose rest for a couple of hours before cutting off the base and trimming the rose underneath.

15 Colour the remaining white chocolate pale green. Roll out the chocolate between 2 sheets of non-stick cooking parchment into a piece large enough to cut out 2 or 3 rose leaves. For authenticity, let the petals dry over the back of a wooden spoon or rolling pin to give them a rounded shape. When the roses and leaves have firmed up, place them on the plate with the cake.

250 g (9 oz) butter or margarine
250 g (9 oz) caster sugar
10 ml (2 tsp) lemon zest
4 large eggs (size 1), weighing 250 g (9 oz)
115 g (4½ oz) plain flour
115 g (4½ oz) potato flour
5 ml (1 tsp) baking powder
30 ml (2 tbsp) dark rum

For the buttercream
4 egg yolks (size 2)
100 g (4 oz) sugar
90 ml (6 tbsp) water
225 g (8 oz) butter, softened
grated zest of 2 lemons

To decorate
900 g (2 lb) marzipan
900 g (2 lb) ready-to-roll fondant icing.
2 m (2 yd) cellophane, 23 cm (9 in) wide (your local florist will almost certainly stock this)
several heads of white lilies (Casablanca and Longie lilies are particularly beautiful and have a gorgeous perfume)
trailing ivy and other small leafed green foliage
small ramekin or other bowl filled with florists' oasis

One word of caution. If you use lilies on your cake be sure to get the florist to pinch out the stamens before you take them. If not you might end up with vivid yellow pollen on your hands, or even worse, on your white icing.

1 Grease and line a 23 cm (9 in) round cake tin. Pre-heat the oven to 180°C (350°F) mark 4.

2 Cream the butter or margarine and half the sugar until light and fluffy. Add the lemon zest and mix in. Separate three of the eggs. Add one whole egg and three yolks one at a time. Keep the egg whites separate. Sift the flour and baking powder together, and add to the mixture a little at a time, taking care not to overbeat the mixture. Mix in the rum.

3 Whisk the egg whites until firm but not dry. Add the rest of the sugar and beat again until the meringue is firm and silky. Slacken the cake mixture by mixing in 30-45 ml (2-3 tbsp) of the meringue. Add the rest of the meringue and gently fold it in using a large metal spoon. Empty the mixture into the prepared tin. Bake in the pre-heated oven for 1-1¼ hours. If you wish, make a small hollow in the surface of the cake before baking. Bake until well risen and golden brown. Leave to cool for 10 minutes before turning out on to a wire rack to cool.

4 To prepare the cake, simply cut off any dome-shaped top to give an even cake, and then slice into as many layers as you wish. Make the buttercream as on page 50. Sandwich the layers together with the buttercream. An alternative would be to spread alternate layers with a good quality lemon curd, in which case you could cut down slightly on the buttercream.

5 Marzipan and ice the cake in exactly the same way as the Baroque wedding cake on page 69. Once the cake is iced, allow it to stand for 24 hours before placing the floral arrangement in position.

7 Fill the ramekin or bowl with the oasis and add water. Take the larger lily heads and arrange them in the centre of the display. Use smaller headed blooms to begin creating points at top left and bottom right. Buds or slightly opened flowers are useful when trying to reduce the display to finer points. The top of the decoration is rounded out with small leafed foliage, whilst the bottom makes use of trailing ivy to continue the design around and off the cake. Before placing the display on the cake, wrap the sides of the ramekin or bowl in a length of cellophane.

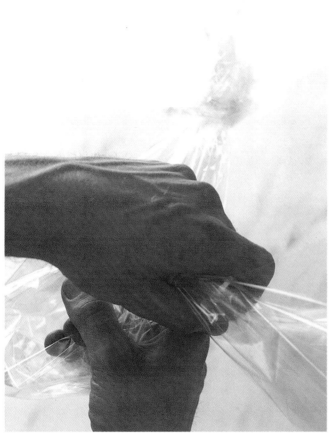

6 Take the cellophane and knot it at intervals down its length. Try to make the spacing between the knots as even as possible. Make sure that the cellophane between the knots is opened out rather than tightly bunched, to provide more reflective surfaces. You will need quite a length of cellophane in the first place, as knotting it tends to use up quite a bit of it. Tie the cellophane around the cake and secure it at the back by either stapling it or using a little sticking tape.

SUNFLOWER CAKE

We did at one time have real grown-up jobs, the kind that see you at your desk by 9am and leaving it by 5pm. That was until we happened upon the world of cake decorating, quite by accident. It turned out to be a very happy accident of course. Never having had any lessons on the subject, I'm sure there were many who asked exactly what our qualifications were. We always thought that it was exactly because we didn't have any formal training, or any hard and fast rules drummed into us, that we tended to look at things differently.

Take flowers for example. Most cake decorators delight in showing off their skill in miniaturising flowers. They are almost always tiny, arranged in formal posies, and in pastel colours. For a brief period we went along with this, until we were asked to judge a cake decorating competition sponsored by a sugar company and a food magazine, and to create a cake to go in the magazine. That is when we hit on the idea of sunflowers.

The theme of the competition was summer, and we created a cake which had life-sized sunflowers shooting out of the top on lengths of green dowel. It was a lovely cake that made everyone smile. It summed up the whole spirit of summer, and encouraged us to look at ways of designing cakes with tiny details blown up large. We are not going to burden you with the detail of how to make sugar sunflowers, but instead take advantage of the variety of sunflowers now available. The sunflowers here had paper heads detachable from the stems.

500 g (1 lb 2 oz) self raising flour, sifted
20 ml (4 tsp) baking powder
good pinch of salt
225 g (8 oz) unsalted butter
400 g (14 oz) caster sugar
6 egg yolks, at room temperature
10 ml (2 tsp) vanilla extract
425 ml (15 fl oz) milk, at room temperature

For the filling
65 g (2½ oz) cornflour
225 g (8 oz) caster sugar
grated rind of an orange
100 ml (4 fl oz) orange juice
45 ml (3 tbsp) lemon juice
50 ml (2 fl oz) water
2 egg yolks (size 2), lightly beaten
10 ml (2 tsp) butter

For the frosting
2 egg whites (size 2), unbeaten
350 g (12 oz) caster sugar
75 ml (5 tbsp) water
2.5 ml (½ tsp) salt
5 ml (1 tsp) vanilla extract
1.25 ml (¼ tsp) cream of tartar

To decorate
2 paper sunflowers
1 m (1 yd) gold ribbon, 1 cm (½ in) wide

1 Grease and line a 25 cm (10 in) round cake tin. Pre-heat the oven to 180°C (350°F) mark 4.

2 Sift the flour with the baking powder and salt. Cream the butter until light and fluffy (this is easier if it is at room temperature to start with). Add the sugar gradually and beat until light and fluffy. Beat in the egg yolks and add the vanilla. Add the flour mixture to the butter mixture, alternating with the milk. Stir the mixture until smooth.

3 Pour the mixture into the prepared tin and bake in the pre-heated oven for about 1¼ hours or until a skewer inserted into the centre comes out clean. This cake rises well and should be firm to the touch. Cool the cake in the tin for 10 minutes before turning out on to a wire rack to cool.

4 To make the filling, combine the ingredients in the order given in a bowl. Place the bowl over a pan of boiling water and cook for 10 minutes, stirring constantly. Allow the mixture to cool. Cut the cooled cake in half and spread the filling between the layers. Place the cake on a serving plate.

5 To make the frosting, if you have a strong food mixer, simply put the ingredients in the bowl and turn the beaters on to full power. Leave for 5-10 minutes until the mixture is thick, creamy and spreadable. Alternatively, put the ingredients in a bowl over a pan of boiling water. Beat constantly for about 7 minutes until the mixture holds a peak. Remove from the heat and beat until cool and spread able. Cover the cake and leave overnight to give the frosting time to dry on the outside.

6 To decorate, fix one sunflower to the board using a little softened marzipan to hold it. Lay the top flower in position with one leaf, and then gently push it into the frosting to fix it. Curl ribbon around the flowers and on to the cake.

7 If you buy silk flowers, place them on the cake in the same way. If using real flowers, some cake decorating shops sell plastic spikes designed to be filled first with water and then with real flowers. You could fill a small container with oasis, wet it, and then arrange the flowers to hide the container.

COFFEE AND WALNUT CAKE

*Several years ago a couple came to us asking for a wedding cake.
Interestingly it was the man who seemed more concerned about the
specifics of the cake in as far as he hoped that it could be like the
coffee and walnut cake that he remembered having as a child. There then
followed a rather odd half hour as he tried desperately to describe
exactly what this cake was like. Not being a cook, or for that matter a
cake maker, it was difficult to come to any firm conclusion about
what he was looking for. Anyway, this is the recipe that we made for
him, and he seemed well pleased. We hope it stirred some pleasant
memories on his special day.*

*The cake filled with the buttercream and decorated with walnuts makes a
delicious teatime treat, but if you want to make it something even more
special then you might prefer to fill and coat the cake with a simply
delicious American frosting. This frosting develops a crisp outer crust whilst
remaining soft inside. In our finished cake we decided to frost it
on a simple but beautiful wooden tray. The tray was made from
distressed wood stained pink. This provided a wonderful colour against
which to set the floral arrangements. We chose two kinds of
lilies largely because of their size, colour and fabulous perfume, with a
counterpoint of a few heads of deep purple anemones. The loose
swirls of the brilliant white frosting are a perfect background for
the flowers, and the whole effect is one of simple elegance.*

175 g (6 oz) self raising flour
2.5 ml (1½ tsp) baking powder
175 g (6 oz) soft margarine
175 g (6 oz) caster sugar
3 large eggs (size 1)
100 g (4 oz) chopped walnuts
22 ml (4 level tsp) instant coffee dissolved in 20 ml (4 tsp)
hot water

For the buttercream
4 egg yolks (size 2)
100 g (4 oz) sugar
90 ml (6 tbsp) water
225 g (8 oz) butter, softened
10-15 ml (2-3 level tsp) instant coffee powder dissolved
in 15 ml (1 tbsp) hot water (optional)

For the American frosting
450 g (1 lb) granulated sugar
150 ml (5 fl oz) water
pinch of cream of tartar
2 egg whites (size 2)
flowers, for decoration

1 Grease and line two 20 cm (8 in) round cake tins. Pre-heat the oven to 170°C (325°F) mark 3.

2 Sieve the flour and baking powder into a large bowl. Add the remaining ingredients and whisk until thoroughly combined. Using an electric hand whisk or mixer is really helpful with this. The mixture should be of dropping consistency. If not, simply add warm water, a couple of teaspoons at a time. Spoon the mixture into the tins and bake in the pre-heated oven for approximately 30 minutes or until a skewer inserted into the centre comes out clean.

3 Allow the cakes to cool in the tins for only a minute or so before turning out on to a wire rack to cool completely. Remove the paper and sandwich together with butter cream.

4 To make the buttercream, beat the egg yolks lightly in a bowl. In a pan, heat the sugar with the water until dissolved and then bring to the boil. Boil until the syrup reaches the soft ball stage or 115°C (239°F) on a sugar thermometer. Gradually pour the hot syrup onto the egg yolks, beating • constantly, and continue beating until the mixture is cool and thick (an electric mixer is helpful for this). Add the butter and whisk again. The buttercream can either be spread between and on the cakes as it is, or to enhance the coffee flavour, add the dissolved coffee powder after adding the butter.

6 Alternatively, to make the American frosting put the sugar and water into a heavy-based pan and heat gently until the sugar has dissolved. Add the cream of tartar. Bring to the boil and continue until the temperature reaches the soft ball stage (115°C/239°F). Meanwhile beat the egg whites until very stiff. Pour the sugar syrup in a thin stream on to the beaten egg whites, beating briskly all the time. Continue beating until the frosting is thick enough to stand in peaks with the ends just tipping over. Spread the frosting between and over the cake, and leave to set.

7 If you want to prepare the flowers in advance, arrange them in a small bowl (or ramekin) filled with florists' oasis and water to keep them fresh. Alternatively, simply arrange the flowers just prior to serving the cake.

A STOLLEN FOR ALL SEASONS

Stollen is a traditional cake eaten in Germany throughout the Christmas period, and appears in various guises in shops and food halls around the world at that time. The sadness is that it too wickedly delicious to confine to so short a time period, and we think should be enjoyed throughout the year. With that in mind we have come up with a lovely recipe for the stollen itself, and four simple but stunning ways to decorate it to accompany the seasons.

Here we have used a 25 cm (10 in) diameter savarin mould that is about 7.5 cm (3 in) deep. If you do not have a mould like this but would like to try the recipe, then you could bake the stollen in the traditional way as explained in step 7.

While we were testing this recipe, two exceptionally talented friends Chris and Harpal, who run the Papillon Pâtisserie in London's Muswell Hill, gave us some fresh yeast to use. They warned us that it was French yeast and somewhat slow-acting. We can now testify that it certainly is slow. Beginning the process at nine in the morning, it was nine in the evening before we were taking the finished stollen from the oven! Perhaps there is a lesson to be learned – maybe good things do take time and patience. However, working on the basis that 'life is too short to stuff a mushroom', we have suggested using fast-acting yeast in this recipe.

**50 g (2 oz) fresh yeast or 3 x 6 g sachets easy
blend yeast
350 ml (12 fl oz) tepid milk
700 g (1½ lb) strong white flour
4 ml (¾ tsp) salt
115 g (4½ oz) butter, softened
grated rind of 2 lemons
50 g (2 oz) chopped mixed peel
100 g (4 oz) glace cherries, halved
175 g (6 oz) currants
175 g (6 oz) sultanas
100 g (4 oz) marzipan, chopped
60 ml (4 tbsp) dark rum
1½ eggs beaten (it is easiest to beat 2 eggs and
use three-quarters of the mixture)
10 ml (2 tsp) sugar
icing sugar, to decorate**

1 If using fresh yeast, crumble it into a bowl and mix with the warm milk and sugar until smooth. Leave for 15 minutes in a warm place to froth. If using dried yeast, read the sachet and continue as advised. Some yeasts do not require mixing with milk and sugar but allow you to empty the dried yeast straight into the flour with the other ingredients.

2 Put the flour and salt into a bowl and rub in 75 g (3 oz) of the butter. Add the lemon rind to the bowl.

3 In another bowl mix the fruit and chopped marzipan and add the rum. Mix well together and allow the fruit to absorb the rum. Add the fruit to the flour along with the eggs, sugar and the yeast mixture. Mix thoroughly to form a soft dough.

4 Turn out on to a floured work surface and knead for about 10 minutes until smooth, adding more flour if the mixture is sticky. Cover with a clean cloth and leave to rise in a warm place for about one hour or until doubled in size.

5 Knead the dough for a further 2 minutes. Rub the remaining butter into the base and up the sides of the mould. Roll the dough gently into a length that will fit inside the mould allowing the edges to join up. To ensure that the edges stick together during baking, brush each end of the dough with a little water and gently push them together.

6 Cover the mould with a clean cloth and leave to rise again for a further 45 minutes or until the dough has almost filled the tin. Pre-heat the oven to 180°C (350°F) mark 4 and bake the stollen for 45 minutes or until well risen and golden brown. Let the stollen rest in the tin for 10 minutes before turning out onto a wire rack. Dredge the buttery surface of the stollen with icing sugar until the butter will not absorb any more. The icing sugar will form a crisp white crust.

7 To bake in the traditional way, simply roll out the dough after it has risen for the first time into an oval approximately 30 x 23 cm (12 x 9 in). Fold one half of the dough on top of the other half, leaving about 2.5 cm (1 in) between the bottom front edge and the top front edge. To ensure that the dough sticks together, brush the surface with either more rum or a little water before folding it over. Cover the folded dough with a cloth and leave to rise as before for 45 minutes. Brush the surface of the stollen with the remaining softened butter and bake as before.

8 The stollen has been decorated to take account both of its depth and its shape. For Christmas it is simply a matter of surrounding the stollen with Christmas baubles and small tree gifts. Equally, it could look particularly stunning with poinsettia heads and holly to offset the frosty whiteness of the icing sugar. Perhaps it would be kinder to use false or silk poinsettia rather than to cut the real plant.

9 For summer, nothing could be easier than to surround the finished item with a wide selection of fruits. When using fruit decoratively remember to combine colours and shapes, and to cut some of the fruit so as to make the best of the insides. This is particularly true of fruits such as pomegranates which are filled with brilliant red or pink seeds. Try to include some fruits like the physalis or Cape Gooseberry that comes wrapped like a Chinese lantern, holding the beautiful golden fruit inside its tissue-like case. Try opening the outer leaves and twisting them to form an umbrella over the fruit. If cutting some fruits in half, leave the stones in one or two. It all adds to the interest.

10 The spring and autumn designs could almost be interchangeable. In one we have taken a series of false fruits and berries bought from a dried flower shop. Some contained grapes, others peaches, whilst others were collections of red berries of different sizes. All these decorations are built on wire so making the final decoration

was simply a case of twisting the various pieces together. As you will see from the photograph, the centre of the decoration is heaviest in detail with the peaches dominating. The fruits then thin slightly to grapes and ultimately taper down to the berries which trail out to a fine point. It is worth noting that the decoration is not absolutely balanced. The berries at one end are much larger than at the other – sometimes having things too balanced can be rather dull. The finished piece is then placed on the top edge of the stollen with the arms of the crescent trailing down and around the sides, without ever touching.

11 The final decoration relies on the simple contrast of two colours. Green and white look so fresh but at the same time dramatic. This decoration was made of several lengths of false variegated ivy wound around the cake. Three full blooms of white Longies lily were then added along with several false buds that tend to add a tapering effect to what might otherwise have become a somewhat bulky decoration.

·Ribbons and Fabric·

the cake onto another board, so that the fabric doesn't actually come into contact with the cake).

In the case of ribbons, these can be used as ribbon inserts as in Aunty Madge's Christmas Cake or even used to wrap otherwise uninteresting cake pillars. This can be an inexpensive but quite gorgeous way of finishing a cake, and the only limit is your ability to imagine. As an idea of how far you can go, we were once asked to create a special cake for a television show that was looking at weddings. At that time we

were
crafts
Venet
were
conce
myste
could
create
style
highly
sugar
been
cake
fine g
masks
myste

RIBBON
S

A deceptively simple way to decorate a cake in no time at all using ribbon insertion.

au
ar
w
w
op
pa
be
ex
ar
w
cc
de

in
in
qu

AUNTY MADGE'S CHRISTMAS CAKE

It often seems to be the case that no matter how much we might collect new recipes, or buy cookery books to widen our range of ideas, at certain times of the year, such as Christmas, we revert to tried and tested old favourites. I suspect that in part this is a way of continuing small family traditions, and remembering times past. We are always glad to go home for Christmas and find Aunty Madge's cake as part of the feast. It's good to remember her.

This cake is decorated using a technique called ribbon insertion. Anyone interested in traditional cake decorating will know that it is a way of using ribbon pushed into icing to give the impression that it is threaded through the icing. In most instances this uses tiny pieces of ribbon and often produces an end result that gets lost amid a mass of other decorations, and whatever else it contributes, it certainly adds nothing in the way of flamboyance. Used our way, you have a quick, simple and inexpensive way of creating a stunning centrepiece. The cake used for the photograph is a 23 cm (9 in) oval which uses the same amount of ingredients as a 20 cm (8 in) round, and is cooked for the same time. This shows that the technique works equally well whatever the shape of cake. If you have never tried this technique before, it is worth choosing stiff ribbon. Soft silk or satin ribbons do not hold the large bows and curls and would simply flop down.

the cake onto another board, so that the fabric doesn't actually come into contact with the cake).

In the case of ribbons, these can be used as ribbon inserts as in Aunty Madge's Christmas Cake or even used to wrap otherwise uninteresting cake pillars. This can be an inexpensive but quite gorgeous way of finishing a cake, and the only limit is your ability to imagine. As an idea of how far you can go, we were once asked to create a special cake for a television show that was looking at weddings. At that time we

were exploring the traditions and crafts of the masks used in Venetian carnival. In particular we were fascinated by the whole concept of the disguise and mystery that wearing a mask could afford the wearer. We created a three tiered American-style cake iced in cream featuring highly jewelled and decorated sugar masks. Once the masks had been fixed in position, the whole cake was then swathed in a very fine gauzy fabric as if to mask the masks. Highly effective, very mysterious and very romantic.

To do this cake justice, it is worth investing in a good quality maple syrup. Beware all those bottles masquerading as the real thing.

AUNTY MADGE'S CHRISTMAS CAKE

It often seems to be the case that no matter how much we might collect new recipes, or buy cookery books to widen our range of ideas, at certain times of the year, such as Christmas, we revert to tried and tested old favourites. I suspect that in part this is a way of continuing small family traditions, and remembering times past. We are always glad to go home for Christmas and find Aunty Madge's cake as part of the feast. It's good to remember her.

This cake is decorated using a technique called ribbon insertion. Anyone interested in traditional cake decorating will know that it is a way of using ribbon pushed into icing to give the impression that it is threaded through the icing. In most instances this uses tiny pieces of ribbon and often produces an end result that gets lost amid a mass of other decorations, and whatever else it contributes, it certainly adds nothing in the way of flamboyance. Used our way, you have a quick, simple and inexpensive way of creating a stunning centrepiece. The cake used for the photograph is a 23 cm (9 in) oval which uses the same amount of ingredients as a 20 cm (8 in) round, and is cooked for the same time. This shows that the technique works equally well whatever the shape of cake. If you have never tried this technique before, it is worth choosing stiff ribbon. Soft silk or satin ribbons do not hold the large bows and curls and would simply flop down.

225 g (8 oz) plain flour
5 ml (1 tsp) baking powder
225 g (8 oz) butter or margarine
225 g (8 oz) demerara sugar
5 eggs (size 2)
225 g (8 oz) raisins
225 g (8 oz) currants
175 g (6 oz) sultanas
100 g (4 oz) glace cherries, halved
pinch of salt
1.25 ml (¼ tsp) ground cinnamon
50 g (2 oz) ground almonds
30 ml (2 tbsp) rum

To decorate
700 g (1½ lb) marzipan
700 g (1½ lb) ready-to-roll fondant icing
2 m (2 yd) ribbon, 4 cm (1½ in) wide (the ribbon must
crease when folded)
1 m (1 yd) gold rope

1 Grease and line a 20 cm (8 in) round cake tin. Pre-heat the oven to 150°C (350°F) mark 2.

2 Sieve the flour and baking powder together. Cream the butter or margarine and sugar until light and fluffy. Beat in the eggs one at a time, following each egg with 15 ml (1 tbsp) of flour. Stir in the rest of the flour. Fold in the fruit, ground almonds, salt and spice. Finally, add the rum and mix well.

3 Spoon the cake mix into the tin and bake for approximately 2½ hours, or until a skewer inserted into the centre comes out clean. Cover the top of the cake during the second half of the cooking time to ensure that it does not become too well done. Cool in the tin. If you want to keep the cake before decorating it, wrap in greaseproof paper and store in an airtight tin.

4 If you want to 'feed' the cake with more alcohol, simply turn the it upside down with the flat side uppermost. Take a cocktail stick and prick the surface all over, going at least a 5 cm (2 in) into the cake. Drizzle the alcohol over the surface, allowing it to sink in before re-wrapping the cake. In our experience many recipes are extremely cautious with their use of alcohol, recommending a couple of tablespoons for the 'feeding'. This really would add very little in terms of flavour. Don't be afraid – add as much as you like. We have found that once the cake is cut, the alcohol hardly ever stands out in its own right, but helps marry all the other flavours together.

5 To marzipan and ice the cake, see page 69 for instructions. Make sure that the plate or base the cake sits on is at least 5 cm (2 in) bigger than the cake to allow for the decoration.

6 The cake should be iced and allowed to rest for at least 12 hours to give the icing time to firm up before decorating. This means that when cuts are made in the icing and the ribbon is inserted, there is no risk of the icing coming away from the marzipan.

7 Wrap the gold rope around the base of the cake. Secure the cut ends either with a small amount of royal icing, or simply cut the rope, allowing the ends to overlap slightly, and then bind them together with cotton before sliding into position over the cake.

8 Take a scalpel or thin bladed sharp knife and make a horizontal cut the same width as the ribbon in the icing directly above the rope. Make another cut the same width as the ribbon 1 cm (½ in) into the top of the cake. Try to make sure that these cuts marry up neatly.

9 Cut the ribbon into 20 cm (8 in) lengths and cut a 'V' shape into both ends for decoration. Fold the ribbon and make a firm crease 5 cm (2 in) from both ends of the piece. The ribbon we used had the pattern in the reverse colours on the other side, so we were able to take advantage of this by turning the ribbon over for each alternate piece.

10 Cut a piece of thin, stiff card the same width as the ribbon and 7.5 cm (3 in) long. Put the card into the crease of the ribbon and gently but firmly press the ribbon into the cut. Pull the card out carefully, leaving the ribbon fixed in position, and then repeat in the cut on the surface of the cake. Continue until you have used all eight pieces of ribbon. When fixed in position, gently curl the ends of the ribbon as in the photograph.

BAROQUE CAKE

For many years Greg worked as a jewellery designer for some of the best known jewellers in London, creating exquisite new pieces and redesigning settings for old ones. In many of the cakes featured in gallery exhibitions that we have held, this knowledge of design and the ability to display a variety of elements in ways that create new effects came to the fore, and in particular enabled us to introduce new materials and ways of working into the field of cake decorating. With this particular cake we have drawn together various decorative elements and worked them together to decorate a basic fruit cake with all the richness of colour and texture that typifies the Baroque period.

This recipe tastes excellent even if you don't have several months to let it mature. Some people swear by leaving the cake for months whilst others believe that there is little to be gained in leaving the cake beyond a few weeks. The choice is up to you. One thing is for sure though – this particular recipe produces a fruit cake that has proven extremely popular with people who used to say that they didn't like fruit cake. The answer may lie in the absence of dark sugars and molasses, and the presence of liberal amounts of brandy. So rather than being overly dark and dry, this simple recipe produces a rich, flavourful and moist cake.

The decoration we used on the top of the cake was a golden wire crown which we embellished with paste jewels and pearls. Any golden decoration would work well, or maybe even an arrangement of candles.

This cake is made of three round fruit cakes measuring 25 cm (10 in), 20 cm (8 in) and 15 cm (6 in).

	25 cm (10 in)	20 cm (8 in)	15 cm (6 in)
mixed fruit	1 kg (2 lb 6 oz)	600 g (1 lb 5 oz)	250 g (9 oz)
glace cherries	150 g (5 oz)	75 g (3 oz)	100 g (2 oz)
mixed peel	100 g (4 oz)	50 g (2 oz)	25 g (1 oz)
ground almonds	100 g (4 oz)	50 g (2 oz)	25 g (1 oz)
ground cinnamon	7.5 ml (1½ tsp)	3.75 ml (¾ tsp)	2.5 ml (½ tsp)
ground mixed spice	5 ml (1 tsp)	2.5 ml (½ tsp)	1.25 ml (¼ tsp)
plain flour	400 g (14 oz)	225 g (8 oz)	100 g (4 oz)
margarine	350 g (12 oz)	175 g (6 oz)	75 g (3 oz)
soft brown sugar	350 g (12 oz)	175 g (6 oz)	75 g (3 oz)
eggs (size 2)	5	3	2
cooking times	3¾ hours	2¾ hours	2 hours

brandy, for 'feeding' the cake (optional)

To marzipan and ice the cake
35.5 cm (14 in) round cake board
25 cm (10 in) thin round cake board
20 cm (8 in) round cake board
15 cm (6 in) round cake board
4 plaster cake pillars
2 kg (4½ lb) marzipan
2 kg (4½ lb) ready-to-roll fondant icing
apricot jam
a little brandy

To decorate
50 cm (20 in) gold net fabric
50 cm (20 in) purple silk fabric
2 m (2 yd) claret rope
3 m (3 yd) claret silk ribbon, 4 cm (1½ in) wide
2 m (2 yd) red satin ribbon, 1 cm (½ in) wide
cotton or string
glue
paste jewels (from a haberdashers)
flat-backed strung pearls
strung pearls
a Christmas decoration

1 Grease the cake tins and line them with a double layer of greaseproof paper. Pre-heat the oven to 150°C (300°F) mark 2.

2 Mix together the dried fruit, halved cherries and mixed peel in a bowl or plastic bag. Add the ground almonds, spices and half the flour. Mix the ingredients in the bowl or toss them in the plastic bag to coat the fruit.

3 Cream the margarine and sugar until light and fluffy. Add the eggs one or two at a time and mix well, adding a tablespoon of flour after each egg. Fold in any flour that remains and then add the dried fruit mixture. Spread the mixture in the tin and level off the top.

4 Tie two or three thicknesses of brown paper or newsprint round the tin with string. Bake the cake in the oven for the time shown. For larger cakes it might be advisable to reduce the oven temperature to 140°C (275°F) mark 1 after half the cooking time, and to cover the top of the tin with a double layer of paper to prevent the surface from overcooking. To test whether the cake is ready, insert a skewer into the centre of the cake. If it is done, the skewer will come out clean. When cooked, allow the cake to cool in the tin.

5 Turn the cake out of the tin and prick the surface all over with a cocktail stick to a depth of 5 cm (2 in). Sprinkle the surface of the cake with brandy or another spirit to 'feed' it. By adding alcohol you are aiding the process of the cake's maturing whilst at the same time adding flavour. As we have said in 'Aunty Madge's Christmas Cake' don't be afraid of adding the alcohol. By the time you marzipan and ice the cake the flavours will have blended together and no one flavour will dominate. Wrap the cakes in greaseproof paper and silver foil and store in a cool place until you are ready to decorate them.

6 Marzipan the large cake on to the 35.5 cm (14 in) board, the medium cake on to the 25 cm (10 in) board, and the small cake on to the 20 cm (8 in) board. Begin by turning the cakes upside down on their respective boards. Roll out a sausage of marzipan and push it into the space left between the cake and the board.

7 Using a flat bladed knife, trim the marzipan to the edge of the cake. Smooth the marzipan to ensure that the sides of the cake are completely flat. Spread the top and sides of the cakes with sieved apricot jam.

8 Roll out the marzipan on a work surface lightly dusted with icing sugar into a circle large enough to drape over the cake and cover it completely. Gently smooth the marzipan on to the surface of the cake, and then with hands lightly coated in icing sugar, smooth the marzipan down the sides of the cake. With a flat bladed knife, trim off any excess marzipan. Smooth the marzipanned surface to ensure that it is as flat as possible. Repeat this process with all the cakes. You will need 900 g (2 lb) marzipan for the larger tier, 700 g (1½ lb) for the middle tier and 450 g (l lb) for the top tier. Leave the marzipanned cakes for several hours, or overnight, before proceeding.

9 When ready to continue, brush the surfaces of the marzipanned cakes with either boiled water or brandy.

10 Roll out the fondant icing on a work surface lightly dusted with icing sugar, until you have a circle large enough to cover the cake. Drape the icing sheet over the cake and smooth it carefully into position on to the top of the cake. When the top is smooth, gently press the icing against the sides of the cake and force it gently downwards until you reach the board. This will force out any air, rather than risk trapping it under the icing. With a flat bladed knife trim off any excess icing. Repeat this process with all three cakes. You will need 900 g (2 lb) icing for the larger cake, 700 g (1½ lb) for the middle tier and 450 g (1 lb) for the top tier. Let the icing dry for 24 hours before assembling the cake.

11 Take the medium cake (the one marzipanned on to the thin cake board) and gently bend the edges of the board down away from the cake. This will have the effect of loosening the icing and marzipan from the board. When you have done this, take a flat bladed knife and slide it under the cake. Gently lift the cake on to the top of the large bottom tier, making sure that it is centred in the middle of the cake.

12 Wrap the edge of the small cake board in the narrow ribbon and secure the ends with glue. Place the board on top of the medium iced cake. Place the cake pillars in position on the board.

14 Take 23 cm (9 in) lengths of the claret ribbon and tie into bows. Fix the bows on to the fabric decoration at the point where the fabric is pinched in with cotton. It is much easier to tie the ribbons off the cake and then fix them later than it is to try and tie them straight on to the length of fabric. Wrap the decoration around the side of the cake and fix at the back by either stapling or taping the ends together. Repeat this on all three cakes.

13 To make the decoration for the sides of the cake cut the fabrics into pieces 15 cm (6 in) wide and long enough to go around each cake with a little to spare. Lay the gold and purple fabric out on a work surface lying next to each other. Put a length of the rope between the two fabrics. Pinch the fabric and rope together at regular intervals, and secure by tying with cotton or string.

15 Wrap the 35.5 cm (14 in) board and the 20 cm (8 in) board in narrow ribbon, and fix with glue. Decorate the boards wrapped in red ribbon with jewels glued around the sides. Glue the flat-backed pearls on to the pillars in a spiral. Glue the strings of pearls around the top edge of the largest board and the 20 cm (8 in) board. Place the top tier on the pillars and add the gold decoration.

MAPLE SYRUP CAKE

Judith lives with her family in Vermont. We first met 25 years ago when we were both working at the same hospital near Livingstone in Scotland and became friends. Although we have only met once more during the intervening 25 years when she visited London, we remain good friends. We may only exchange Christmas cards, and send photos with updated family histories, but I know that if we were to meet again tomorrow, within minutes it would seem that it had only been a matter of days since we last spoke. Over a cup of tea and a slice of cake we would find what it is that keeps us friends.

Knowing of our interest in cakes, and love of food generally, Judith once sent us a beautiful can of the most delicious maple syrup, a product for which the state of Vermont is rightly famous. It was a real treat to pour that gorgeous amber liquid over waffles and pancakes, and to taste the true flavour of maple. She also sent a lovely recipe leaflet with cake recipes, one of which we share with you here. Next time Judith comes to London, or maybe when we are passing through Vermont, a slice of maple syrup cake will have to feature on the menu.

This recipe calls for quite a lot of maple syrup, and in fact its success depends upon you buying a good one. It is worth spending that bit extra and buying pure maple syrup as opposed to maple 'flavoured' syrup which is not the same thing at all. Fortunately some supermarkets are now selling the real thing as a regular item, and so the price is coming down. We baked two of these 23 cm (9 in) cakes to give us extra depth,

sandwiched them together, and then covered them with this absolutely
delicious frosting. If you prefer to settle for baking just one cake,
you will only need half the amount of frosting. The frosting has a
beautifully silky texture that is a delight to use. Unlike some
other frostings, it doesn't thicken too quickly as it cools or as you continue
to work it. Instead, it stays soft with a pale ivory colour and delicate
sheen. It would work just as well with the coffee and walnut cake.
It is worth noting that the frosting stays soft to the touch for several hours
after it has been applied. If you are going to use ribbons or fabric
to decorate the cake, it would be best to leave it for 6-8 hours to allow the
surface to dry slightly. It will then be possible to touch, but
only delicately as too heavy a hand will leave fingerprints and may
slightly discolour the finish.

For a special teatime treat, why not try simply studding the sides of the
cake with walnut halves? For a more elaborate centrepiece we have
chosen to 'wrap' the cake in ribbons and gauzy fabrics. We concentrated
on four major colours, dark and pale blue, deep lavender and gold.
The fabrics were loosely drawn together into a rosette, creating volume by
adding large curls and folds. The rosette arrangement was then loosely
tied together and secured with cotton before being fixed on to the
top surface of the cake using a cocktail stick. Then simply arrange the
remaining ribbons and fabric down and around the sides of the
cake, creating visual interest by twisting them in and around each other.

100 g (4 oz) margarine
100 g (4 oz) caster sugar
2 eggs (size 2)
65 ml (2½ fl oz) water
225 ml (8 fl oz) maple syrup
350 g (12 oz) plain flour
1.25 ml (¼ tsp) bicarbonate of soda
10 ml (2 tsp) baking powder
2.5 ml (½ tsp) ground ginger (optional
50 g (2 oz) chopped walnuts (optional)

For the frosting
225 ml (8 fl oz) maple syrup
2 egg whites (size 2)
pinch of salt
5 ml (1 tsp) vanilla essence or extract

1 Grease and line a 23 cm (9 in) round cake tin. Pre-heat the oven to 170°C (325°F) mark 3.

2 Cream the margarine and sugar until light and fluffy. Mix the water with the eggs and then beat lightly. Add the beaten eggs a little at a time, followed by the maple syrup. Sift together the flour, bicarbonate of soda and baking powder. Stir the flour into the egg mixture a little at a time until thoroughly mixed in. If you wish, add the ground ginger and chopped walnuts to the mixture.

3 Pour into the prepared tin and bake in the pre-heated oven for 45-50 minutes or until a skewer inserted into the centre comes out clean. Turn out on to a wire rack and leave to cool.

4 To make the frosting, gently boil the syrup until it reaches 115°C/239°F (soft ball stage) on a sugar thermometer. Remove from the heat and cool slightly whilst you whisk the egg whites with a pinch of salt, until firm but not dry. Add the syrup to the eggs in a fine stream, beating all the time. An electric mixer is really useful here. Continue until the frosting holds its shape. Add the vanilla and use to spread in and over the cake.

SEVENTEENTH CENTURY FRUIT CAKE

Several years ago we were fortunate enough to receive a copy of Sara Paston-Williams book, 'The Art of Dining – A History of Cooking and Eating'. It is a wonderful book that charts the huge changes in food production, cooking methods and entertaining from the Medieval and early Tudor period to the Victorian and Edwardian times. It also contains some wonderful recipes taken from works of the period such as the adapted recipe that follows. This fruit cake recipe was originally found in Elizabeth Birkett's Commonplace Book of 1699. Seventeenth century cakes were often huge as Elizabeth Birkett's list of ingredients indicates: 'Take 3 pound and a halfe of flower, 2 pound and a halfe of Currans, halfe a pound of Raisons of your sun stoned, halfe a pound of sugar, halfe a pint of rose watter, a pint of Creame, a pound of fresh butter, a Gill of Ale barme, yolks of 10 eggs and 3 whites'. The resulting mix was then piled on to buttered paper and baked in the cooling bread oven.

By the end of the century cakes were becoming slightly more symmetrical in that they were being cooked inside tin hoops to ensure a more even rise. However they were cooked, these cakes were delicious by any standards. This recipe is no exception and we have decorated it to reflect the gaiety and grandeur of the time. This cake would be a wonderful idea for anyone looking for something out of the ordinary, and

because it is neither iced nor marzipanned it avoids any unnecessary
sweetness. This recipe produces a lovely fruity and moist cake that would
be perfect served at a reception in the afternoon, perhaps with tea, or
would be equally at home on a more elegant occasion, perhaps served
with a spiced wine or mulled ale, consistent with the period.
It is interesting to note that rose water appeared in many recipes of the
period in place of ordinary water, which was often of dubious quality.
The cakes have been wrapped in a twisted collar of paper ribbon and
topped with a variety of silk flowers, once again concentrating
on the use of claret and cream. We deliberately chose larger blossoms, but
also included some that would allow trailing points to be built into the
design. The larger flowers are peonies and lilies whilst the smaller
ones are freesias. From a purely practical point of view, this would make
an ideal wedding cake in that it would save time, not requiring
weeks or months of maturing, and the floral decoration could be made in
advance. Also, when buying silk flowers you are assured that
they will be perfect on the day, and you will be able to keep them
as long as you wish.

2 eggs (size 2)
2 egg yolks
100 g (4 oz) caster sugar
pinch of salt
375 g (13 oz) butter, melted
215 ml (7½ fl oz) double cream
45 ml (3 tbsp) rose water
300 ml (10 fl oz) warm water
550 g (1 lb 4 oz) plain flour
2 x 6 g sachets easy-blend dried yeast
10 ml (2 tsp) ground mace
450 g (1 lb) currants
225 g (8 oz) raisins

For the glaze
15 ml (1 tbsp) caster sugar
15 ml (1 tbsp) rose water
15 ml (1 tbsp) butter

To decorate
1 m (1 yd) cream-coloured paper ribbon
1 m (1 yd) claret-coloured paper ribbon
selection of silk flowers
florists' oasis

1 Grease and line a 25 cm (10 in) round cake tin, and wrap with a double layer of brown paper or newsprint around the outside. Tie with string.

2 Beat the whole eggs with the extra egg yolks, the sugar and the salt until thoroughly combined. Mix in the melted butter and gradually beat in the cream, followed by the rose water and water. Stir in the flour, yeast, mace and dried fruits and mix well. Cover with a piece of oiled plastic wrap and leave to prove in a warm place for about 30 minutes.

3 Pre-heat the oven to 180°C (350°F) mark 4. Pour the mixture into the prepared tin and bake in the centre of the oven for 1¼-1½ hours or until a skewer inserted into the centre comes out clean. If necessary, cover the top with a layer of brown paper after 30 minutes to prevent the top from browning too much.

4 To make the glaze, dissolve the sugar in the rose water over a low heat, then stir in the butter. Brush over the cake immediately after removing it from the oven. Leave to cool in the tin. Wrap in greaseproof paper and foil and leave to mature for at least 24 hours before cutting.

5 For our photograph we have made two cakes, the smaller one measuring 15 cm (6 in) round and made using half the ingredients listed for the 25 cm (10 in) tin, and cooked for 50-60 minutes. The two cakes are then placed one on top of the other. There is no need to worry about supporting the smaller tier as these cakes are sufficiently dense to withstand the weight.

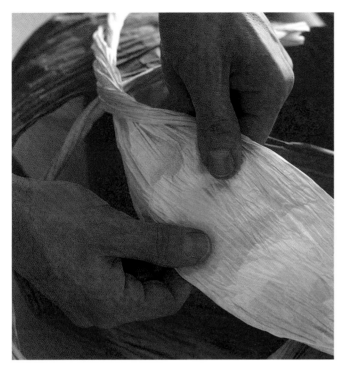

6 The larger cake has been wrapped in two shades of paper ribbon – claret and cream. This particular ribbon is widely available and is tightly bound like rope when first bought.

7 Unwind the ribbon and then simply twist the two colours together into a collar that will fit around the bottom tier. Secure the ribbon together by either stapling the two ends together or sticking them with tape. Slide the collar into position around the cake.

8 Fill a small ramekin with dry florists' oasis (the kind used for dried or silk flowers) and make up the centre of the design using four or five large peony heads. Extending out of the top left of the design, add smaller peony heads and a large spray of freesia curled around at the top. To balance this, coming out of the bottom right of the design, place some smaller lilies with trailing buds. Bend these round and down to the left to echo the curve of freesias at the top. Position the display in the centre of the top tier and place the whole cake on a simple but elegant fluted silver plate.

✦ Fruit ✦

FRUIT

Soft, red and yielding, this particular heart is studded with succulent raspberries.

We never cease to be amazed by the huge range of products that modern shops and supermarkets seek to provide. It was probably not that long ago that fruit was available in the greengrocers only during the local growing season. The idea that something could be shipped or flown from another continent, arrive in perfect condition and still be affordable would have seemed impossible.

And yet this small miracle happens every day, week in, week out. New items, or new to us that is, appear regularly. Horned melon, persimmon, guava, cherimoya, papaya, passion fruit and mango sit beautifully side by side with our home-grown apples and pears,

The velvety texture of cheesecake makes a beautiful contrast to the juicy slices of orange.

2

strawberries and blackberries, plums and gooseberries. We are fortunate to be able to share in the exquisite tastes and experience the exotic flavours and perfumes of these fruits, but do we ever stop to fully appreciate the beauty of these items before we cut into them and enjoy them?

We believe that eating starts with the eyes. We first attract the attention of diners with a sight of what they are about to appreciate. In this way we can help them anticipate what is to come, and to enjoy it before they get their first taste. Fruit can be used in this way. We have chosen several recipes that either feature fruit as an important part of the recipe, or as an additional 'layer' of flavour that sits well with a particular cake. We have tried to choose some fruits which are easily available and hopefully showed how intrinsically beautiful they are, or can be.

Layer upon layer of melting meringue and the softest sponge are piled on a thick filling of strawberries and cream.

6 The effect you are looking for is a heart-shaped cushion, so you will need to shape the edges so that they slope gently down from the top to the bottom edge of the cake. When you are satisfied with the shape of your heart, transfer it to your serving plate.

5 To decorate the cake, cut out a circle of greaseproof paper the size of your cake tin. Then draw as large a heart shape as possible within the circle. Place the paper heart on top of the cake and, using a sharp knife, cut out a heart shape. The cut edge will form a 90 degree angle to the top of the cake.

7 You will see from the finished photograph that we decorated our cake on a wicker basket. This offered us an interesting background texture as well as a warm pale colour to offset the depth of the raspberries. Spread sieved raspberry jam over the surface of the cake and then cover with raspberries. As a final detail we made a delicate white frill of gypsophila around the cake to add a touch of lightness.

SHAKER APPLE CAKE

At Manchester, in England,

This blessed fire began,

And like a flame in stubble,

From house to house it ran:

A few at first receiv'd it,

And did their lusts forsake;

And soon their inward power,

Brought on a mighty shake.

This little jingle refers to the birth on 29th February 1736 of Ann Lees who, at the age of 22, joined a group of dissenters in Bolton, near Manchester. It was this same uneducated textile worker and cook who eventually became the leader of her religious community, finally leaving England to set sail for America, where she and her followers arrived on 6th August 1774. We are more likely to know of the Shakers now as a result of their beautiful furniture and food. In both cases, the Shaker philosophy of simplicity and the bounty of nature are evident. This lovely cake recipe with its delightful, and surprising frosting, comes from that simple, excellent tradition.

The cake pictured in the photograph is made up of two apple cakes, covered in frosting and decorated with red apple slices. For an added touch of colour, use green eating apples as well as the red varieties to decorate the cake.

75 g (3 oz) butter
175 g (6 oz) soft dark brown sugar
1 egg (size 2)
175 g (6 oz) plain flour, sifted
pinch of salt
10 ml (2 tsp) baking powder
150 ml (5 fl oz) milk
2.5 ml (½ tsp) ground cinnamon
3 medium eating apples (approximately 450 g (1 lb),
peeled and chopped

For the apple frosting
1 cooking apple (approximately 175 g (6 oz))
225 g (8 oz) caster sugar
5 ml (1 tsp) ground cinnamon (optional)
1 egg white (size 1)

To decorate
1 dessert apple
10 ml (2 tsp) lemon juice

1 Grease and line a 20 cm (8 in) round tin. Use non-stick cooking parchment as ordinary greaseproof paper pulls pieces of apple out of the cooked cake. Pre-heat the oven to 180°C (350°F) mark 4.

2 Cream the butter and half the sugar together until light and fluffy. Beat the remaining sugar with the egg and add to the first mixture. Sift in the flour, salt, baking powder and cinnamon alternately with the milk. Add the apples and mix.

3 Pour the mixture into the prepared tin and bake for 45-50 minutes or until firm to the touch, and a skewer inserted in the centre comes out clean. Let the cake cool in the tin for 10 minutes before turning out on to a wire rack.

4 To decorate, peel and core the cooking apple and cook gently with a tablespoon of water until soft. When cool, push the pulp through a fine sieve. Put the cooked apple, caster sugar, cinnamon and egg white into the bowl of an electric mixer. Beat on high speed until the mixture is thick, white and creamy. It is possible to do this by hand, but it requires patience and a strong wrist. You can use eating apples in the frosting, but in our opinion the result is a little too sweet.

5 If using two cakes, use a little frosting to stick them together. However, don't use too much as the cake is quite dense and the frosting rather soft. If you use too much frosting it will squeeze out of the sides, making the shape of the finished cake look a little odd. Use the rest of the frosting to cover the top and sides in generous swirls.

6 To continue the Shaker theme, we have frosted the cake on a wooden board. The cake is then decorated in wafer thin slices of whole eating apple. If you have a mandolin or kitchen gadget that cuts fruit in varying thicknesses, simply wash the apples and slice as thinly as possible. Try to retain the detail of the core and the pips as you cut through the centre. If you do not have a mandolin, cut the apples by hand, but make the slices as thin as possible. To prevent the apples discolouring, brush them with lemon juice before applying to the sides and top of the cake. This touch of acidity also works well with the sweetness of the frosting.

TWO-TIER CHEESECAKE

Without fail, every time we visit a restaurant or plan a dinner party

menu, we always start at the end, that is with the pudding.

A meal is somehow incomplete for us if there isn't the promise of

something rather wicked at the end of it. One of our all-time favourites

has to be a cheesecake, but definitely not the kind that makes your

spoon bounce into the air when you try to take your first

mouthful, having been made with gelatine, nor the kind that is puffed up

with whisked egg whites into little more than a mousse which disappears

all too quickly on the tongue. The ideal cheesecake, from a

purely personal viewpoint, should have a thick and creamy layer made

up of simple but good ingredients, should be firm without

being stodgy but sticks your tongue to the roof of your mouth. Bliss!

The following recipe combines all the essential 'ingredients', and

produces a cake that is sufficiently grand for any occasion.

The cheesecake itself is a beautiful cream colour when sliced. It has a

slight vanilla flavour and would sit well with any fruits. It is

also delicious served with an accompanying sauce. In our orange version

a simple sauce was created by sieving bitter orange marmalade and then

adding a little hot water to thin it. Alternatively, add a favourite liqueur

of your choice such as Cointreau or Grand Marnier.

For our photograph we have baked a second tier measuring 15 cm (6 in)

using half the quantities given for the 23 cm (9 in) cake and reducing the

cooking time to approximately 40 minutes.

For the shortbread crust
225 g (8 oz) plain flour, sifted
100 g (4 oz) granulated sugar
1 egg yolk (size 1), beaten
100 g (4 oz) butter, softened

For the filling
450 g (1 lb) cottage cheese
450 g (1 lb) cream cheese
350 g (12 oz) granulated sugar
4 eggs (size 1), lightly beaten
25 g (1 oz) cornflour
30 ml (2 tbsp) lemon juice
5 ml (1 tsp) vanilla extract
100 g (4 oz) butter, melted
450 ml (15 fl oz) sour cream

To decorate
sliced oranges
bay leaves
sieved orange marmalade

1 Put the flour and sugar in a bowl and make a well in the centre. Add the beaten egg yolk and softened butter, and blend into the dry ingredients. Using your hands, mix everything thoroughly. The warmth of your hands should draw everything together into a ball of dough. Wrap in cling film and chill for 10 minutes.

2 Pre-heat the oven to 200°C (400°F) mark 6.

3 Take a 23 cm (9 in) round springform cake tin and press the shortbread dough into the bottom of the tin. Don't bother trying to roll it out – it is far easier simply to spoon the mixture into the tin and, using the back of the spoon, press the dough into a smooth base. If the dough is slightly crumbly this will make life a lot easier. Try to make the layer in the tin approximately 5 mm (¼ in) thick, and evenly distributed. This makes the finished crust look more elegant, but more importantly is the right amount of crust in relation to the filling.

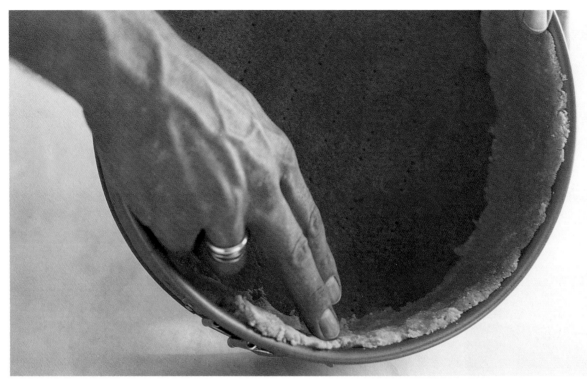

4 Prick the crust all over with a fork and bake in the pre-heated oven for 15-20 minutes or until golden. Allow to cool before pressing the rest of the shortbread evenly against the sides of the tin. For simplicity's sake, turn the cake tin on its side and simply press the dough down to meet the base and up to the top of the tin. Don't worry if this feels a bit messy. The sides are not going to be pre-baked, and if they look a little uneven this will be covered up once the filling is added.

5 Pass the cottage cheese through a sieve. In a large bowl beat together the cottage cheese and cream cheese until well mixed. Add the sugar and eggs and mix until blended. Add the cornflour, lemon juice and vanilla extract, and beat until smooth. Add the butter and sour cream and mix until just blended. Pour the mixture into the prepared crust. Place the tin on a baking sheet and bake at 150°C (300°F) mark 2 for approximately 2 hours, or until the cake is firm at the edges and slightly browned. Allow to cool and then chill. Note that when taking the cheesecake from the oven the centre may look rather wobbly. As long as the edges are set,

the centre will firm up as it cools. Do not be tempted to continue cooking until the centre is firm as this will almost certainly dry it out.

6 Remove the cake from the tin and place on a serving plate. Remove the smaller cake from its tin and place on a thin 15 cm (6 in) round cake board. If you want to stack the cakes as we have, simply cut four lengths of dowel rod (you can buy special cake decorating ones at cake supply shops). Each length should be as deep as the cake plus 2.5 cm (1 in). Simply push them through the cake until you feel the base. Arrange the rods in a square so that you can then sit the smaller tier on top. This cake is sufficiently deep and firm (particularly having been chilled in the fridge) that it can easily support the top tier.

7 In our finished cake we have emphasised the simplicity of the cake's own colours – two shades of gold – by slicing whole oranges and overlapping them on the top and bottom tier interspersed with bay leaves. The oranges are glazed with sieved orange marmalade.

SUMMER STRAWBERRY MERINGUE CAKE

It seems odd to think that the strawberry that we all enjoy so much today did not actually appear until about 1821. Of course, before that there were a variety of types available, ranging from wild strawberries to those imported from the colonies of Virginia, and from as far away as Chile. It used to be the case that strawberries enjoyed a relatively short season, and that by mid to late summer the best was over, and that we would have to wait patiently until the next year. Now, with modern transportation making the world a much smaller place, strawberries appear throughout the year. Despite that, it always seems that the home-produced fruits appearing in early summer are the most delicious, perhaps because they herald the beginning of those long golden days. This summer strawberry meringue cake is a lovely creation with layers of yellow sponge and creamy white meringue above and below the classic combination of strawberries and cream.

This mixture makes an extravagantly deep cake which looks even more wonderful if served on a cake stand to give more height. Using a loose-bottomed or spring-sided cake tin makes life easier.

We have been told that this cake tastes even better the day after it has been made. I'm afraid that we can offer no useful guidance on this point as the cake never lasts that long in our house!

For the sponge
50 g (2 oz) margarine
100 g (4 oz) caster sugar
2.5 ml (½ tsp) vanilla essence
4 egg yolks
100 g (4 oz) plain flour
5 ml (1 tsp) baking powder
45 ml (3 tbsp) milk

For the meringue
4 egg whites
225 g (8 oz) caster sugar
50 g (2 oz) flaked almonds

To decorate
300 ml (10 fl oz) double cream
fresh strawberries

1 Pre-heat the oven to 180°C (350°F) mark 4. Grease and line two 20 cm (8 in) round cake tins.

2 To make the sponge, cream the margarine and sugar together until light and fluffy. Add the vanilla essence, followed by the egg yolks one at a time. Beat well after adding each egg yolk.

3 Sift the flour and baking powder together and fold into the egg mixture, lightly but thoroughly, alternating with the milk. Divide the mixture between the tins and spread the mixture evenly using the back of a spoon.

4 To make the meringue, whisk the egg whites until stiff but not dry. Add half the sugar and whisk again until stiff and glossy. Sprinkle on the remaining sugar and fold into the meringue. Divide the meringue between the tins and level the tops. Sprinkle one of the meringue surfaces with almonds and bake the cakes in the pre-heated oven for 45-50 minutes or until the cakes have shrunk slightly from the sides of the tin. Turn out carefully onto a wire rack and leave to cool, meringue side down.

5 To fill the cake, whisk the cream until it begins to hold its shape. Spread the cream on the cake without the almonds, and decorate with sliced strawberries. Reserve 5 or 6 of the best fruits for the top of the cake. Put the remaining half of the cake in position and decorate using the whole strawberries.

• Weddings •

WEDDINGS

Pavlova – a light and melting end to any celebration.

Hopefully a wedding day will be a day to remember for the rest of a couple's life. In the past few years we have met quite a lot of prospective brides and grooms, and have been fortunate enough to meet those who were looking for something different, something out of the ordinary. It was often amusing to let them see our portfolio of designs and the books we had written. It was obvious that, at least to begin with, they had a fixed idea of what they should be looking for. Sometimes planning a wedding cake would take a couple of meetings, as the first one was taken up with trying to get rid of preconceived ideas, and simply to illustrate what was possible. Once they got the idea, they would often come up with some wonderful suggestions of

Lazy swirls of piped frosting are offset by the gold chopped nuts and a scattering of apricot roses.

their own.

These days we hardly make any cakes, unless they are a special commission. Instead we prefer to show people how to create something stunning and personal for themselves. It is undoubtedly true that weddings can be hugely expensive, and all too often people get swept along in doing things 'by the book'. It seems that somebody somewhere has published a list of what is necessary in order to create the perfect wedding. A cake is on the list, and so there has to be a cake. Well, if there has to be a cake, at least let it be a delicious one. Why not choose a cake that, rather than just being something tagged on to the end of a meal, is an integral part of the feast? The cakes in this chapter are certainly a great deal less expensive than the average wedding cake, and almost certainly a great deal more tasty.

Making and decorating a wedding cake is nowhere near as difficult as it might at first seem. Have a try. You will surprise yourself, and at the same time create a lasting memory of that special day.

A pile of panettones bound to attract everyone's attention.

FRANCATELLI'S GRAND FRUIT CAKE

According to our friend Glynn Christian, this recipe was devised by the great Francatelli for Queen Victoria while he was working at Buckingham Palace. It might appear similar to many fruit cakes in its construction, but the ingredients differ sufficiently to make this a lovely fruity surprise. Do not be tempted to forego any of the mixed peel as it really does add to the citrus appeal. Orange flower water can be bought at delicatessens and larger supermarkets. It might even be worth trying the pharmacist, but make it clear you need it for culinary purposes. Most Indian or Middle Eastern shops stock it.

The design was a request from a winter bride, who wanted her cake decorated with deep red roses, holly and ivy, and the whole cake swathed in claret velvet to match the bodice of her dress. The effect was both dramatic and romantic, and this is a simplified version using tartan.

The flowers used are quite hardy, and do not need to be in water. However, if the cake might be on display for some time, arrange them in wet florists' oasis in small bowls. The nightlights would be attractive at an afternoon or evening reception in winter. This cake was baked in hexagonal tins measuring 25 cm (10 in), 20 cm (8 in) and 15 cm (6 in) across, using 2½ times the mixture divided between the tins. You can also use round tins with the above diameters, using the same amount of cake mix. Cooking times hardly vary.

350 g (12 oz) butter or margarine
225 g (8 oz) caster sugar
4 eggs (size 2), beaten
350 g (12 oz) plain flour
pinch ground cloves
450 g (1 lb) currants
175 g (6 oz) sultanas
175 g (6 oz) mixed peel
100 g (4 oz) glace cherries, halved
100 g (4 oz) ground almonds
2.5 ml (½ tsp) ground nutmeg
2.5 ml (½ tsp) cinnamon
finely grated rind and juice of 2 oranges and 1 lemon
30 ml (2 tbsp) orange flower water
120 ml (8 tbsp) brandy

To decorate
2 kg (4½ lb) marzipan
2 kg (4½ lb) ready-to-roll fondant icing
sieved apricot jam
35 cm (14 in) hexagonal cake board (measured between opposite flat sides)
25 cm (10 in) hexagonal cake board
20 cm (8 in) hexagonal cake board
20 cm (8 in) round cake board
15 cm (6 in) round cake board
8 plaster wedding cake pillars
50 cm (20 in) tartan fabric, cut into 3 lengths each 15 cm (6 in) deep
2 m (2 yd) matching tartan ribbon, 2.5 cm (1 in) wide
1 m (1 yd) red ribbon, 1 cm (½ in) wide
6 deep red open roses
bunch of holly
ivy
nightlights (optional)

1 Grease and double-line the tins with greaseproof paper, and wrap the outside of the tins with a double thickness of brown paper or newsprint secured with string. Pre-heat the oven to 150°C (350°F) mark 2.

2 Cream the butter and sugar together until light and fluffy. Add the eggs one at a time, following each egg with a tablespoon of flour. Add the rest of the flour, leaving 175 g (6 oz) to use with the fruit.

3 Put the mixed fruit, peel, glace cherries, ground almonds, the remaining flour and the spices into a plastic bag. Hold the neck of the bag closed and shake to coat the fruit with the flour, almonds and spices. Tip the fruit into the cake mix and stir until well combined. Finally, add the rind and juice of the lemon and orange along with the orange flower water and brandy.

4 Divide the cake mixture between the tins and smooth the surface. Bake the large cake for 1½ hours before turning the heat down to 130°C (250°F) mark ½ and continue cooking for a further 1½ hours. For the middle tier, cook for 1¼ hours at the higher temperature and a further 1¼ - 1½ hours at the lower temperature. For the small cake, cook for 1¼ hours at the higher temperature and a further 1¼ hours at the lower temperature. In all cases when you have reduced the temperature, cover the tops of the cakes with a sheet of brown paper or newsprint to prevent the surfaces from over-browning. Test the cakes with a skewer to see if they are done. Allow the cakes to cool in the tins before removing them and wrapping in greaseproof paper and foil prior to decorating.

5 Marzipan and ice each cake as the Baroque wedding cake (see page 69), using the same amounts of marzipan and icing for the three tiers. The only difference is the shape of the cake, and the fact that the hexagons produce folds of marzipan and icing at each point of the cake. The marzipan is slightly more difficult to smooth out around the cake, however if you proceed as described in the Baroque cake, gently stretching the marzipan down the sides of the cake, you should achieve a completely flat surface. If you find

folds of marzipan that you cannot smooth out simply cut them off neatly with a flat bladed knife close to the cake to preserve flat surfaces. By smoothing the newly applied marzipan it is possible to even out any irregularities.

6 The icing is easier to apply due to its being softer. Do not forget to brush the surface of the cakes with either alcohol or boiled water before putting the icing on the cake, other wise it might not stick in position. Once the cakes are iced, leave them for 24 hours before proceeding.

7 Take the tartan fabric and fold down the cut edges so that they are behind the main piece. Take pieces of the tartan ribbon and tie them around the fabric at intervals. Wrap the ribbon around the fabric a couple of times, overlapping the ribbon so that it looks like a cross at the front. Secure the ribbon with staples or cotton. Repeat this along the length of the fabric, then tease out the fabric between the knots so that it billows out. Wrap these lengths of tartan around the respective cakes and secure at the back using either staples or cotton.

8 Wrap the edges of the round boards in the narrow red ribbon, and fix with a little glue. Place the larger round board on top of the bottom tier, and place four of the cake pillars on top of it. Place the smaller round board on top of the middle tier, and place the remaining four pillars on top of it. Stack the cakes as in the photograph.

9 The flowers and holly and ivy are then loosely arranged between each set of pillars, and on top of the cake. Arrange the nightlights at the base of the cake.

CARROT CAKE

The cab driver rang the door bell and I made my way to the door with the wedding cake. It was a three-tiered creation arranged in the American style made out of carrot cake and covered in a shimmering white meringue with curling piping. We were rightly proud of our creation. The driver looked anxious. I explained that all he need do was drive carefully, and be gentle when taking corners. To reassure myself, I had supported each layer on lengths of dowel rods so that during transport the cakes would not sink down and disturb the meringue.

No sooner had we reached the end of the road, and after a somewhat sharp right turn, I noticed that the bottom tier had moved slightly. We then entered the only road in Camden with seven 'sleeping policemen' and proceeded to hit them all as if we were Damon Hill in search of a Grand Prix win. By now I was up to my wrists in meringue. The cake was ruined. I very calmly explained to the driver that I needed to arrive as soon as possible as repair work was necessary. This might have been a mistake. The pressure meant that we got hopelessly lost and I arrived at the reception minutes before the bridal party. I quickly got rid of the meringue and spread the cake with whipped cream. I took a plastic carrier bag, filled it with the remaining cream and snipped off one corner.

This improvised piping bag allowed me to repeat my lazy curling piping before disappearing down the back stairs whilst the bride came up the front stairs. We subsequently received a letter of thanks for the cake which was 'perfect'.

	15 cm (6 in)	20 cm (8 in)	25 cm (10 in)
eggs (size 2)	1½	2	3
caster sugar	150 g (5 oz)	175 g (6 oz)	250 g (9 oz)
sunflower oil	175 ml (6 fl oz)	225 ml (8 fl oz)	350 ml (12 fl oz)
lemon juice	10 ml (2 tsp)	15 ml (1 tbsp)	25 ml (1½ tbsp)
self raising flour	150 g (5 oz)	200 g (7 oz)	300 g (11 oz)
salt	2 ml (⅓ tsp)	2.5 ml (½ tsp)	3.75 ml (¾ tsp)
cinnamon	2 ml (⅓ tsp)	2.5 ml (½ tsp)	3.75 ml (¾ tsp)
bicarbonate of soda	2 ml (⅓ tsp)	2.5 ml (½ tsp)	3.75 ml (¾ tsp)
baking powder	4 ml (¾ tsp)	5 ml (1 tsp)	7.5 ml (1½ tsp)
ground cloves	pinch	pinch	pinch
grated carrot	175 g (6 oz)	225 g (8 oz)	350 g (12 oz)
pineapple chunks, drained and finely chopped	175 g (6 oz)	225 g (8 oz)	350 g (12 oz)
chopped walnuts	40 g (1½ oz)	50 g (2 oz)	75 g (3 oz)
dark rum	25 ml (1½ tbsp)	30 ml (2 tbsp)	45 ml (3 tbsp)
cooking time	50-60 minutes	1-1¼ hours	1-1¼ hours

For the cream cheese frosting (quantity for decorating one tier)

75 g (3 oz) butter, softened
2.5 ml (½ tsp) vanilla essence
75 g (3 oz) cream cheese
175 g (6 oz) icing sugar

To decorate

275 g (10 oz) chopped mixed nuts
35 cm (14 in) round cake board
17.5 cm (7 in) thin round cake board
25 cm (10 in) thin round cake board
cake pillars
dowel rods

1 Grease and line the cake tins. Pre-heat the oven to 180°C (350°F) mark 4.

2 Place the eggs and sugar in a bowl and whisk until pale and thoroughly creamed. Add the oil in a thin stream, whisking all the time until you get a thick creamy mixture. Add the lemon juice.

3 Sift the flour and remaining dry ingredients on to the egg mixture and mix. Stir in the carrots, pineapple and walnuts and mix. Stir in the rum. Turn the mixture into the tins and bake in the oven for the times given or until risen, brown and firm to the touch. Cool on a wire rack.

4 Place the bottom tier of the cake on a plate or board which will allow room for the piping around the bottom edge and any flowers. Place the middle tier on a thin board. Once this tier has been covered in cream and nuts you will be moving it on to the top of the bottom tier. Place the top tier on the cake board.

5 To make the cream cheese frosting, mix together the butter and cream cheese, and add the icing sugar a little at a time until you have a smooth creamy mixture. To decorate the three tiers you will probably need three times this amount. Using a spatula, coat the top and sides of the cakes with the frosting. Save some frosting for piping.

6 Toast the nuts. Place them in two batches in a non-stick frying pan over a gentle heat. Shake the pan now and again to ensure that the nuts are an even colour. Be careful not to let them burn. Tip them on to a clean plate. Do not leave them in the hot pan to cool down as cooking will continue and the nuts become darker.

7 Take a small handful of cold toasted nuts and gently press them against the sides of the cakes in turn. Try to cover the sides as completely as possible. Be careful that your hands don't get too sticky, or the nuts will stick to you instead.

8 Slide a knife under the middle tier of the three cakes and gently place it in position on top of the bottom tier. Try to make sure that it is positioned in the centre. Fill a piping bag fitted with a small star nozzle with the remaining cream cheese mixture, and pipe small scrolls around the cakes.

9 The top tier is then supported on four hollow cake pillars. These pillars do not take the weight of the cake, but simply cover four lengths of dowel rod. The thickness of the rod will depend on the pillars you buy. Cut the dowel to a length that is the height of the two bottom tiers plus the height of the pillar. Cut four pieces to this length. Place the pillars in position on top of the middle tier and then push the dowel rods through the pillars and down into the cake until you meet the board or plate.

10 Once the dowel rods are in position, slide on the pillars and place the top tier on the pillars. Decorate with flowers of your choice. We used a beautiful dark apricot rose and placed the flower heads fairly randomly over the cake, and scattered some of the petals on to the cake and around it.

PANETTONE

Like brioche, panettone is a wonderfully simple but absolutely delicious cross between a bread and a cake. Originally from Milan in northern Italy, it is most often found packaged in beautiful boxes, hanging from the ceilings of Italian delicatessens. The actual shape and texture of the cake is just as pleasing as the taste, and it occurred to us that it would make a rather smart wedding cake. The lightness of the cake with its beautiful buttery flavour would be elegant if served by itself, and would certainly make an exciting change from the rich fruit cake that many people expect. However, like the lemon pound cake, it is also a cake that one could 'marry' up with different flavours, for example poached fruits or fruit salads and fruit sauces. In this way the cake becomes a delicious part of the dessert.

To reproduce the traditional shape of the panettone, we have baked them in terracotta flower pots. Prepare the pots for baking by soaking them in water overnight. The quantity of ingredients given here is for a pot with a 15 cm (6 in) interior diameter at the top, and a height of 15 cm (6 in).

450 g (1 lb) plain white flour
1 x 6 g sachet easy-blend dried yeast
300 ml (10 fl oz) warm milk
175 g (6 oz) softened butter
1 egg and 4 yolks (size 2)
75 g (3 oz) caster sugar
finely grated rind of 1 lemon
finely grated rind of 1 orange
75 g (3 oz) candied peel, chopped
100 g (4 oz) raisins
pinch grated nutmeg

To decorate
raffia
oranges
dried fruits
cocktail sticks

1 Sift the flour into a large bowl and sprinkle over the yeast. Make a well in the centre and pour on the milk. Mix with a knife to form a soft dough. Knead on a floured work surface for 5 minutes, then replace in the bowl. Cover with oiled cling film and leave in a warm place for 45 minutes-1 hour or until doubled in size.

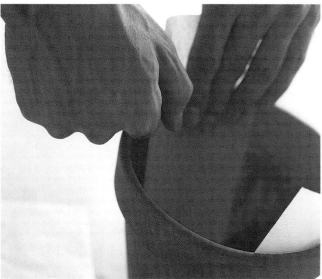

2 Meanwhile, prepare the terracotta pot. Wash it thoroughly and then grease the inside. Cut several pieces of non-stick cooking parchment and use to line the inside of the pot.

3 Knock back the dough. Add the rest of the ingredients to the bowl and mix well with your hands until a reasonably smooth mixture is achieved.

4 Put the mixture into the lined pot and leave in a warm place for 1 hour or until it rises above the top of the pot.

5 Pre-heat the oven to 200°C (400°F) mark 6. Beat the whole egg and use to brush the top of the panettone. Bake in the oven for 20 minutes, and then lower the temperature to 180°C (350°F) mark 4 for a further 40 minutes or until a skewer inserted in the centre comes out clean. Allow to cool for about 10 minutes before turning out of the pot to cool completely. The panettone should be stored in an airtight tin for no more than a week.

6 The remaining tiers of the cake are made in one 18 x 18 cm (7 x 7 in) pot, one 12.5 x 12.5 cm (5 x 5 in) pot and one 10 x 10 cm (4 x 4 in) pot. The largest plant pot requires 1½ times the amounts quoted for the above recipe, and the two remaining pots are filled using the amounts given above, but split between the two pots. Cooking times as follows:

18 cm (7 in) pot: 1-1¼ hours at 180°C (350°F) mark 4. Cover the top during cooking to avoid over-browning.
12.5 cm (5 in) pot: 10 minutes at 200°C (400°F) mark 6, then 30 minutes at 180°C (350°F) mark 4.
10 cm (4 in) pot: 10 minutes at 200°C (400°F) mark 6, then 20-25 minutes at 180°C (350°F) mark 4.

If you do not wish to use terracotta pots, the cake can be baked in a 15 cm (6 in) round tin for 15 minutes at 200°C (400°F) mark 6, then 40 minutes at 180°C (350°F) mark 4.

7 To assemble the cakes, take the largest panettone and remove a round section from the risen dome of the cake, leaving a flat surface large enough to sit the next size of panettone on top of it. Continue in this way with all the panettones until the four tiers are safely assembled. The cakes should stand without wobbling, and should need no support. However, if you want to be absolutely sure, cut a length of wooden dowel the same height as the pile of panettones, and simply press the dowel rod down through the cakes until you feel the board they are sitting on.

8 To finish the cake, wrap each tier in raffia bows (the raffia can be bought from some florists or from craft supply shops). Using a cannel knife, cut swirling patterns of peel from whole oranges, and then arrange the peel cascading down the cake from top to bottom. The pieces of peel are held in place with a cocktail stick. The patterned oranges are then piled around the base of the cake with one on top. The decoration is then finished with bundles of cinnamon sticks, fir cones, gold Christmas decorations, dried bay leaves, dried limes and pomegranates and whole nuts in their shells.

PAVLOVA WEDDING CAKE

Many years ago, Max's grandmother Ruth went to Australia to visit her daughter and other members of the family. She came back with colourful stories to tell, not least of which was of a wonderful pudding called a pavlova. It was many years later, whilst sharing a flat with two Australian girls, that we first laid eyes on this wonderful confection – a pale golden pile of crisp meringue with a thick layer of white marshmallow inside, topped with thick double cream and sumptuous fruits of the season. From that point on the recipe became a firm favourite.

All those years ago, grandmother Ruth also told stories of how, in Australia, pavlovas were piled on top of each other and served at weddings. We have been intrigued by this notion ever since, particularly as we couldn't think of a way to stack these wonderfully soft and delicate creations without ending up with a huge mess. The answer eventually proved wonderfully simple, and although it might not be the way things are done in Australia, it provides a 'cake' with the same classic lines as a traditional wedding cake, but with the surprise of a light and melting end to any celebration.

	20 cm (8 in)	23 cm (9 in)	25 cm (10 in)
egg whites (size 2)	4	5	6
caster sugar	225 g (8oz)	275 g (10 oz)	350 g (12 oz)
sifted cornflour	7.5 ml (1½ tsp)	10 ml (2 tsp)	12.5 ml (2½ tsp)
vanilla essence	2.5 ml (½ tsp)	2.5 ml (½ tsp)	5 ml (1 tsp)
malt vinegar	3.75 ml (¾ tsp)	5 ml (1 tsp)	7.5 ml (1½ tsp)
double cream	300 ml (10 fl oz)	450 ml (15 fl oz)	750 ml (1¼ pints)
milk	15 ml (1 tbsp)	30 ml (2 tbsp)	45 ml (3 tbsp)

To decorate

fruits in season

flowers

ivy

florists' tape, florists' wire or cotton

1 Pre-heat the oven to 100°C (225°F) Mark ¼. Grease and line the base and sides of the springform tin with cooking parchment.

2 In a large mixing bowl whisk the egg whites until they form stiff peaks. Sprinkle over 100 g (4 oz) of the sugar and continue beating until the mixture is very stiff and glossy. Fold in the remaining sugar along with the cornflour, vanilla essence and vinegar.

3 Spoon the mixture into the prepared tin, making sure that the surface is flat.

4 Bake in the pre-heated oven for 2 hours. Turn off the oven and allow the pavlova to cool completely in the oven.

5 Remove the tin from the oven and do not worry if the crust seems to have cracked and collapsed. This often happens and it does not affect the taste or the eventual look. In fact, if the crust has remained intact, take a sharp pointed kitchen knife and gently cut through the crust just inside the top edge of the pavlova and push the crust down inside the tin until it rests on the marshmallow underneath.

6 Pour the double cream into the mixing bowl and add the milk. Whisk until firm peaks form. With the pavlova still inside the cake tin, spoon the cream into the centre. Spread it carefully until the cream topping is completely smooth and level with the top of the crust sides. Once filled with cream, let the pavlova rest in its tin for approximately 30 minutes.

7 Remove the sides of the tin and peel away the lining paper. Remember that the pavlova is quite delicate, and whilst if it should crumble or crack it would not be any less delicious, try to keep it as perfect as possible. To this end you might decide not to remove the base lining paper, but simply to place the pavlova on its serving platter.

8 The stand on which the pavlovas are displayed is a dinner plate stand intended for stacking plates. Many cake decorating supply shops and some cookware shops hire out cake stands that work in the same way. The stands allow the cakes to be stacked without the need for cake pillars and are therefore ideal for the pavlovas. When the three pavlovas have been placed on their respective plates, decorate the stand itself. Take lengths of variegated ivy for each 'leg' of the cake stand and fix them in position with either lengths of florists' wire, florists' tape or even cotton. When the ivy is in position, thread rosebuds, gypsophila or any other flowers of your choice between the ivy leaves.

9 Place the pavlovas on the decorated stand and arrange rose petals and pieces of fruit on each layer and around the edges of the plates. You often see the tops of pavlovas loaded with fruit but on this occasion, in order to retain a classic line, it might be better to place a large bowl of fruit by the side of the cake stand and serve additional fruit with each slice. If you pile too much fruit on top of the pavlovas, the pressure of the fruit could cause the sides to break.

PARSNIP AND LEMON CAKE

*Thane Prince is one of our favourite cookery writers, and this cake is
adapted from one of her recipes that we saw in a newspaper
several years ago. It caught our attention initially because of its use of the
often maligned parsnip. We love parsnips, and in particular
when they are simply cooked in milk until soft and then mashed.
The taste is wonderful and the sweetness a revelation. Our friend
Michelle Berriedale Johnson first introduced us to this way of cooking
parsnips and we pass on the idea whenever possible. The combination of
the sweetness of the parsnip with the flavour of lemon makes
for a delicious cake. Our finished cake is made up of three different sized
cakes, measuring 25 cm (10 in), 20 cm (8 in) and 15 cm (6 in).
The largest cake is made using the ingredients quoted, but cooked in a
25 cm (10 in) tin for the same length of time. We used two cakes this size
in order to give a deep bottom tier. The smallest cake is made up using
half the ingredients quoted, and cooked in a 15 cm (6 in) tin
for the time quoted.
The bottom tier is surrounded by several small arrangements of daffodils
in bowls with dampened florists' oasis. The remainder of the cake
simply has daffodil heads arranged around it. It is a good idea to wrap
the cut end of the flower in either cling film or foil to prevent any
moisture coming into contact with the cake. Finish the decoration by
adding mimosa to offer a difference in colour and texture.*

275 g (10 oz) plain flour
10 ml (2 tsp) baking powder
250 g (9 oz) caster sugar
2.5 ml (½ tsp) salt
4 eggs (size 2)
grated rind of 2 large lemons
30 ml (2 tbsp) lemon juice
5 ml (1 tsp) vanilla essence
225 ml (8 fl oz) vegetable oil
275 g (10 oz) parsnip, finely grated

For the filling
200g (7 oz) cream cheese
225 g (8 oz) icing sugar
5 ml (1 tsp) grated lemon rind
a little lemon juice if necessary

For the frosting
2 egg whites (size 2), unbeaten
350 g (12 oz) caster sugar
45 ml (3 tbsp) water
30 ml (2 tbsp) lemon juice
2.5 ml (½ tsp) grated lemon rind
paste food colouring (optional)

To decorate
35.5 cm (14 in) round cake board
30 cm (12 in) thin round cake board
25 cm (10 in) thin round cake board
1.5 m (1½ yd) yellow gold ribbon, 1 cm (½ in) wide
daffodils
mimosa
florists' oasis

1 Grease and line two 20 cm (8 in) sandwich tins. Pre-heat the oven to 180°C (360°F) mark 4.

2 Sift together the flour, baking powder, sugar and salt. In a large bowl beat the eggs with the lemon rind and juice and vanilla essence, then beat in the oil. Fold in the flour and the parsnips. Divide the mixture between the prepared tins and bake in the pre-heated oven for 35-40 minutes. The cakes should be nicely risen, golden brown and just shrinking from the sides of the tins. Allow to cool briefly in the tins before turning out on to a wire rack to cool completely.

3 Mix the ingredients for the filling together until smooth, adding a little lemon juice if the mixture is too stiff to spread. Once the cakes are cooled, cut into layers and spread with a lemon cream filling. You will need twice this amount of filling for a three tier cake. This filling can also be used to coat the cake as well if you prefer.

4 Place the large cake on the large board, and the two smaller ones on the thin boards.

5 To make the frosting, if you have a strong food mixer, simply put the ingredients in the bowl and turn the beaters on to full power. Leave for 5-10 minutes until the mixture is thick, creamy and spreadable. If you do not have a food mixer, put the ingredients in a bowl over a pan of boiling water. Beat constantly for about 7 minutes until the mixture holds a peak. Remove from the heat and beat until cool and spreadable. Use to cover the cake. You will need twice the amount of frosting given if you wish to cover all three cakes.

6 For an extra touch we shaded the frosting differently for each tier. The bottom tier was a deeper yellow, the middle tier a pale yellow, and the top tier was left white. Spread each tier of the cake in frosting, making sure that you have a even covering. Let the cakes rest on their respective boards for several hours until the frosting feels dry to the touch.

7 Wrap the edge of the bottom board in the gold ribbon and fix in place with a little glue or tape. Take the middle tier and slide a large flat bladed knife underneath the cake. Gently lift it into position on top of the bottom tier, making sure that it is centred. Repeat with the small cake on top of the middle tier. These cakes are sufficiently dense not to require additional support from dowel rods. They may sink very slightly into the frosting due to the fact that it is dry on the outside but remains soft and creamy inside. When the cakes are in position, arrange the daffodils.

ORANGE AND ALMOND CAKE

On a recent trip around London's Soho, we spent some time looking at

two of that area's famous pâtisseries and were drawn by some

lovely cakes that appeared to be covered in what looked like piped

marzipan. In our experience, marzipan is something that people either

love or hate. We had it in mind to include our orange and almond

cake in this book, and began to think that this would be a perfect way of

decorating it. It would continue the almond theme, whilst at the

same time adding a textural dimension to the finished cake. The

particular piped almond mixture that we came up with is a delicious

alternative to marzipan which complements the cake and means that it is

not necessary to add an additional sweet layer in the form of icing or

frosting. This would make a lovely wedding cake, but would also grace

any other special celebration.

Our finished cake was made using two 25 cm (10 in) cakes and one of

18 cm (7 in) diameter as well. The smaller cake was made using half the

quantities given for the larger cake and a slightly shorter cooking time of

approximately 35-40 minutes.

225 g (8 oz) plus 45 ml (3 tbsp) caster sugar
6 eggs (size 2), separated
grated rind of 2 oranges
175 ml (6 fl oz) strained freshly squeezed orange juice
2.5 ml (½ tsp) almond extract
100 g (4 oz) ground almonds
225 g (8 oz) self raising flour, sifted
pinch of salt
225 g (8 oz) unsalted butter, melted and cooled
225 g (8 oz) orange marmalade, sieved

For the piped almond mixture
400 g (4 oz) ground almonds
100 g (4 oz) caster sugar
6 egg yolks, size 2
60-75 ml (4-5 tbsp) rum
1 egg white

1 Grease and line a 25 cm (10 in) round cake tin. Pre-heat oven to 180°C (350°F) mark 4.

2 Whisk together 225 g (8 oz) of the sugar with the egg yolks until thick and pale yellow. Beat in the orange rind and juice and almond extract. Stir in the ground almonds and then beat in the flour.

3 In a separate bowl, beat the egg whites to soft peaks. Add the salt and the remaining sugar and beat until stiff but not dry. Quickly fold the melted butter into the cake mix a little at a time, until completely incorporated. Gently fold the beaten egg whites into the cake mix.

4 Pour the mixture into the prepared tin and bake for 45-50 minutes. The cake should be firm to the touch when cooked or until a skewer inserted into the centre comes out clean. Let the cake cool in the tin for 10 minutes or so before turning out on to a wire rack to cool completely.

5 To assemble the cake, spread sieved orange marmalade between the cakes to continue the orange flavours. As the cake needs to return to the oven when piped, we decided against using an orange buttercream between the cake layers. Although it would probably have been quite safe to do so, we did not want to risk the possibility of the cream beginning to melt at the edges.

6 To make the almond mixture, mix the ground almonds with the sugar, egg yolks and rum until soft enough to pipe. You may need to add some of the egg white to get the mixture to this stage. Spread some of the mixture over the top and sides of the cake, and put the rest into piping bag. Pipe the mixture over the cake. In our finished cake, given its increased size, we needed 1½ times the amounts quoted. If you prefer to use one 25 cm (10 in) cake, then the amounts quoted will be sufficient.

7 Using a 1 cm (½ in) star nozzle, pipe a cross on the top tier. Fill in each quarter of the cross with chevrons, or upside down 'V' shapes, to the edge of the cake, and then pipe a circle of simple star shapes around the top edge. Pipe a series of vertical lines around the sides of both tiers, and once again pipe simple star shapes on the exposed surface of the bottom tiers. To finish the cake add some simple scrolls around the bottom of the bottom tier and around the top edge.

8 Pre-heat the oven to 240°C (475°F) mark 9. Return the finished cake to the oven for a few minutes until the almond layer turns a pale golden colour. Although it is obvious, this is a very hot oven, and you should keep a close eye on the cake to make sure that it doesn't begin to burn. It should also be noted that the surface you have placed the cake on, for example cake plate or cake board, should be able to withstand these temperatures. We decorated the cake on a 1 cm (½ in) silver cake drum, like those traditionally used for icing wedding cakes. This showed no signs of burning when placed in the oven with the cake on it.

9 To complete the cake, glaze the top of the top tier, and the top of the bottom tier with sieved orange marmalade to give a shimmering contrast to the rest of the piping. The oranges with the leaves add a simple finishing touch.

INDEX